# Unlocking Mysteries of God's Word

## Second Edition

## Bill R. Swetmon

Seaside Press

**Library of Congress Cataloging-in-Publication Data**

Swetmon, Bill R.
   Unlocking mysteries of God's word / Bill R. Swetmon. -- 2nd. ed.
      p.   cm.
   Includes bibliographical references and index.
   ISBN 1-55622-036-7 (pbk.)
   1. Bible--Theology.    2. Theology, Doctrinal.    I. Title.
   BS543.S94    1995
   230--dc20                                                    95-37323
                                                                   CIP

Copyright © 1996, Bill R. Swetmon.

Foreword by F.W. Mattox, Ph.D.

All Rights Reserved

ISBN 1-55622-036-7
10 9 8 7 6 5 4 3 2 1
9510

All inquiries for volume purchases of this book should be addressed to
Wordware Publishing, Inc., at 1506 Capital Avenue, Plano, Texas 75074.
Telephone inquiries may be made by calling:

(214) 423-0090

Dedicated to
Linda
A constant companion,
a faithful wife,
a loving mother,
a caring servant
in whom the Lord delights;
and so do I

# Contents

Make your ear attentive to wisdom,
Incline your heart to understanding;
For if you cry for discernment,
Lift your voice for understanding;
If you seek her as silver,
And search for her as for hidden treasures;
Then you will discern the fear of the Lord,
And discover the knowledge of God.

Proverbs 2:2-5

# Foreword

As a beginning Bible student I was shocked to hear a highly respected Bible teacher say that "we must believe both sides of contradictory statements of the Bible." I thought that an all-wise God was a better communicator than to allow any contradictions in His revelation. As I learned more I began to find these opposing statements in the Bible and struggled for years to try to find a basis for a faith which could include them all. I didn't find much help.

In this study by Bill Swetmon, we have that much needed help in building such a faith. He cuts through long and tedious arguments to express clearly and biblically the opposing views and works out skillfully the Christian's response of faith in each instance.

This is not a book to read lightly at one sitting. Each chapter will bring you back for reexamination of ideas and statements, but the result is worth the effort.

And what is the result?

The reader will find an increased knowledge and appreciation of God's method and purpose in His revelation of His acts and plan for man's redemption. He will develop a deeper faith that the Bible is indeed the revelation of God's plan for man's redemption, and his trust and love for God and Christ Jesus our Redeemer will grow.

The word "antinomy" is not in common use in the average vocabulary, but with Bill Swetmon's clear explanation of its meaning, one sees that it is the most meaningful word available to describe these biblical contradictions, both sides of which are true and both to be accepted by faith.

We are indebted to Brother Swetmon, not only for pointing out these many antinomies, but for his leading us to the biblical understanding of how each seemingly opposing side is a part of God's eternal purpose for man's redemption.

If, after reading a chapter, one finds he still does not grasp the full understanding of all the mysteries of Deity, please be reminded that God's ways are above man's, and the day will come when we shall know all things as we are also fully known. In the meantime, this gives room for the growth of faith.

F. W. Mattox, Ph.D.
Chancellor, Lubbock Christian College
Author of *The Eternal Kingdom*

# Chapter 1
# Beginning the Journey

The farm on which I grew up in Kentucky contained a great mystery. There was a large cave on that farm that held great intrigue to the inquisitive mind of a curious farm boy. Many times I would slip off from the house (against the wishes of my parents) to explore the mysteries of the "forbidden" cave. Now there are certain essentials that one needs to explore a cave adequately, such as a good flashlight (with spare batteries), a pick or small shovel, a rope, and perhaps some water and food Spelunking (the science of cave exploration) requires much preparation and forethought in order to prevent disaster. As I look back on those boyhood experiences in that cave, I realize that I took great chances at times because of a lack of preparation. I now see the wisdom of my parents in forbidding me to enter the cave alone. However, the lure of the mysterious clouded my judgment.

In many ways the Bible is like that cave. It is full of mysteries and intriguing adventures. There is a great temptation for one to plunge into it without adequate preparation. The science of hermeneutics was developed in order to adequately prepare one to enter the Bible with the proper tools in order to explore its mysteries. The purpose of this study is not to establish principles of hermeneutics.

Rather our purpose is to establish a base from which one may deal adequately with the divine mysteries that are found in God's Word. The approach is simple, so simple, in fact, that it has been overlooked by a great many people over the years. The results have been obvious in the religious confusion and contradictions that are apparent among Bible-believing people.

There is no question about the fact that the Bible contains mysteries. As a matter of fact, we may expect to find many difficult things in God's Word. " 'For My thoughts are not your thoughts, neither are your ways My ways,' declares the Lord, 'For as heavens are higher than the earth, so are My ways higher than your ways and My thoughts than your thoughts' " (Isaiah 55:8, 9). With finite minds we enter into the Bible which contains a revelation of the infinite. We can expect to be challenged beyond the limit of our understanding. Dr. J. I. Packer wrote, "All theological topics contain pitfalls for the unwary, for God's truth is never quite what man would have expected."[1]

## Avoiding the Pitfalls

The great question which we face is how do we avoid the pitfalls? The solution begins with faith. We must approach the Bible with implicit faith that it is God's Word. Genesis begins with this simple yet very profound statement, "In the beginning God created the heavens and the earth" (Genesis 1:1). Two important facts are set forth in this verse. (1) God exists. He was there in the beginning before anything or anyone else existed. (2) God acted. He created. He brought into existence that which did not previously exist. The acceptance of these two facts will make the remainder of the Bible relatively easy to believe. If one believes that God exists and that God acts, there will be very little difficulty accepting what God says about how and why He acts.

The purpose of this study is not to establish reasons for believing that God exists, that He acts, and that the Bible is His revelation. There are many good books that deal with these issues. If the reader has difficulty accepting these truths about God, this material will be of little value. However, this study will provide a tool for apologetics. It will give an insight into why many non-Christians have trouble believing the Bible.

This study, therefore, is for those who have faith in God and His Word. This is the first step in avoiding the pitfalls.

## What Are the Mysteries?

Almost every revelation from the mind of God contains great mysteries. This in fact is good evidence that the Bible is of divine origin. If man had written the Bible, apart from divine inspiration, he would have endeavored to explain the mysteries so they would be more acceptable to the human mind. The Bible is full of mysteries and difficult statements that man would never have dreamed up. As a matter of fact, most of the Bible's revelation is against man and what man believes and how man lives. It opposes man at almost every turn. Therefore, it would be difficult to believe that man would even write such a book, much less fill it full of difficult mysteries that are unexplainable.

God's revelation often goes beyond human comprehension by setting forth two facts which are both true and yet seem to contradict each other. This is called an *antinomy*. The *Shorter Oxford Dictionary* defines an antinomy as a contradiction between conclusions which seem equally logical, reasonable, or necessary. The point is, there are facts set forth in the Bible that appear to contradict one another. Quoting again from Dr. J. I. Packer:

> An antinomy exists when a pair of principles stand side by side, seemingly irreconcilable, yet both undeniable. There are cogent reasons for believing each of them; each rests on clear and solid evidence; but it is a mystery to you how they can be squared with each other. You see that each must be true on its own, but you do not see how they can both be true together.[2]

## The Problem Illustrated

Figure 1, on the next page, is an illustration of the problem. The letter A represents a divine truth such as the divinity of Christ. We know that A is true because numerous passages set forth this fact without question. However, the letter B also represents a truth that is set forth in Scripture with equal force, such as the humanity of Christ. A sufficient number of Scriptures can be gathered that will support B. The problem is that both A and B are presented as true, yet there seems to be a contradiction because it is hard to comprehend how both facts can be true.

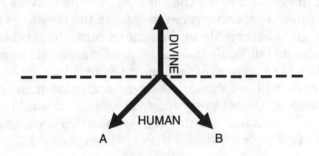

*Figure No. 1*

The horizontal line represents the great gulf between the finite and the infinite. The single vertical line above the horizontal line represents the perfect unity or oneness of God. What appears to the human mind as contradictory is not so with God. If we could see things as God sees them, there would be total unity and harmony in all areas. So the problem with divine mysteries exists only in the limitations of the human mind.

Even though there is a great gulf between the human and the divine, God can still communicate to us, and to a point we are able to comprehend that communication. However, there is a point at which we must accept God's message by faith without the benefit of human reasoning and understanding. This does not mean that the basic doctrines of the Bible are not clear. Every doctrine is set forth in precise order and there can be no question that the doctrine is taught as fact. The problem arises when we find another doctrine in Scripture that seems to contradict the first one.

In figure 1 you will note that lines A and B are closer at the top than at the bottom. This illustrates that the more we learn about these antinomies, the closer we come to understanding the divine mind. Although we may never see the full scope and unity of contradictory doctrines, nevertheless, we can expect to find them less and less troublesome the closer we come to the divine mind. We may even discover ways in which the contradictions can be harmonized in some cases, such as the antinomy of grace and works (chapter 7).

Here, then, is the incentive for diligent study and research. The more we explore the marvelous revelation of the divine mind, the closer we will come to seeing things as God sees them.

## Beware of Extremes

The greatest problem we have with the antinomy is the temptation to go to an extreme by accepting either A or B as true and rejecting the other. This lack of balance can lead to error and a rejection of God's divine truth.

This can be illustrated historically with the antinomy of the God-man revelation about Jesus Christ.

*The Gnostics*. Error arose in the first century concerning the incarnation of Jesus Christ. The Gnostics believed that all matter was evil, so they did not believe that God could live in a flesh-and-blood body. The consequence of this doctrine would be to deny the humanity of Christ. They said that Jesus only "seemed" to live in a human body. He was just a phantom, a divine spirit that manifested Himself in the form of a man.

*Arius of Alexandria*. In the early fourth century a man named Arius who lived in Alexandria, a presbyter and teacher in the church, developed a philosophy that rejected the deity of Christ. Arius said that Jesus was not actually divine but that He was from a high order of created beings, perhaps the highest of all created beings. According to Arius neither true humanity pertains to the Son, for He is without a human soul, nor true divinity, for He is without the essence and attributes of God. The conflict started by Arius eventually led to the Council of Nice or Nicaea in A.D. 325. The council affirmed that Jesus, the Son of God, is "consubstantial" with His divine Father and "consubstantial" with human beings. The word they used may pose a theological problem in its own definition; however, the council

5

was endeavoring to restore a biblical concept and for that effort they are to be commended.

*Eutyches*. During the fifth century a new viewpoint was developed which said that Jesus was neither truly human nor truly divine, but that He was a "tertium quid" (a "third other").

*Socinians*. The swing back and forth between these two parts of Scripture continued through the centuries. In the sixteenth century a group called the Socinians arose to deny the deity of Christ in favor of His humanity.

As you can see from these illustrations, serious problems arise when we fail to keep a proper balance with regard to both truths. The error comes in when man's reasoning is put in place of God's revelation. It is of utmost importance that we accept by faith the full scope of God's revelation without rationalizing or disregarding that which we don't understand.

## Avoiding Sectarianism

In the Lord's Prayer recorded in John 17, Jesus prayed for unity among His followers. "I do not ask in behalf of these alone, but for those also who believe in Me through their word; they may all be one; even as Thou, Father, art in Me and I in Thee, that they also may be in Us; that the world may believe that Thou didst send Me" (verses 20, 21). The unity for which Jesus prayed is destroyed when there is a failure to maintain a proper balance in the antinomy.

A good example is the sovereignty of God and man's free will. Ultra-Calvinism is the concept that God is in complete control of His creation (a concept which is in accordance with biblical revelation). Those who subscribe to this doctrine may neglect the other part of the antinomy, man's responsibility before God. The other extreme is ultra-Arminianism, which is an overemphasis on human responsibility almost to the exclusion of God's sovereignty and divine election.

It is easy to understand sectarianism when we are able to recognize an imbalance with regard to these antinomies. A sectarian, therefore, is identified by his doctrinal stance rather than his association with Christ. The disciples were called Christians because they were identified with Christ (Acts 11:26). There are 20,781 organized churches and denominations worldwide. Of these, 7,889 are Western Protestant proper, approximately 9,950 are nonwhite indigenous Protestant, and 1,345 are marginally Protestant.[3] No doubt there are many factors (population growth, global expansion, cultural differences) that have contributed to the growth and diversity of Protestant denominationalism around the world. However, on closer examination of the doctrinal differences that exist among these churches, one of the things that will surface will be a lack of balance among the biblical antinomies, which has resulted in an overemphasis in one particular doctrine almost to the exclusion of the opposite truth in the antinomy. Therefore, a sectarian church becomes identified with a peculiar doctrinal stance. That doctrine becomes the creed. Fellowship is usually limited only to those who find agreement in the extreme.

So the question arises: How do we avoid these extremes that lead us into sectarianism? Dr. J. I. Packer has the answer:

> What should one do, then, with an antinomy? Accept it for what it is, and learn to live with it. Refuse to regard the apparent inconsistency as real; put down the semblance of contradiction to the deficiency of your own understanding; think of the two principles as, not rival alternatives, but, in some way that at present you do not grasp, complementary to each other. Be careful, therefore, not to set them at loggerheads, not to make deductions from either that would cut across the other (such deductions would, for that very reason, be certainly unsound). Use each within the limits of its own sphere of reference (i.e., the area delimited by the evidence from which the principle has been drawn). Note what connections exist between the two truths and their two frames of reference, and teach yourself to think of reality in a way that provides for their peaceful coexistence, remembering that reality itself has proved actually to contain them both. This is how antinomies must be handled, whether in nature or in Scripture. This, as

I understand it, is how modern physics deals with the problem of light, and this is how Christians have to deal with the antinomies of biblical teaching.[4]

The following chapters will deal with some of the most serious antinomies which have led to religious division and sectarianism over the years. I believe you will find this study to be faith strengthening as together we explore the mysteries of God's divine revelation.

## Notes

[1]J. I. Packer, *Evangelism and the Sovereignty of God* (Downers Grove, IL: Inter Varsity Press, 1961), p. 18.

[2]Ibid., p. 19.

[3]David Barrett, ed., *World Christian Encyclopedia: A Comparative Study of Churches and Religions in the Modern World, AD 1900-2000* (Nairobi: Oxford University Press, 1982), pp. 792-93, 796-97.

[4]Packer, pp. 21-22.

## Remembering the Facts

1. What is an antinomy? Why is it difficult to see the unity in antinomies?

2. What is a great incentive for diligent Bible study and research?

3. What is the greatest danger in connection with the biblical antinomies?

4. Give a brief explanation of the following views in connection with the antinomy of Jesus as God and man:

Gnostics:

Arius of Alexandria:

Eutyches:

Socinians:

5. Why did Jesus pray for unity (John 17)?

6. How is sectarianism identified?

7. How many organized churches and denominations exist worldwide?

8. What are some of the factors that may have contributed to the growth and diversity of Protestant denominationalism?

9. In most cases, why do these doctrinal differences exist among the denominational churches?

10. How do we avoid the extremes that lead to sectarianism?

## Discussing the Issues

1. Why is it so tempting to go to extremes in the various areas of biblical revelation?

2. Why do most dedicated religious people strongly oppose those who disagree with them on biblical matters?

3. What steps can each Christian take to bring about unity, first in the local congregation and then among religious friend and other churches?

4. Why do you think God allows His revelation to contain what appear to be contradictions, without some explanation about them?

# Chapter 2
# God—Three or One?

Then God said, "Let Us make man in Our image, according to Our likeness" (Genesis 1:26).

Hear, O Israel! The Lord our God, the Lord is one! (Deuteronomy 6:4).

"I can't believe that!" said Alice.

"Can't you?" the Queen said in a pitying tone. "Try again; draw a long breath, and shut your eyes."

Alice laughed. "There's no use trying," she said, "one can't believe impossible things."

"I daresay you haven't had much practice," said the Queen. "When I was your age, I always did it for half-an-hour a day. Why, sometimes I've believed as many as six impossible things before breakfast."[1]

## Believing Impossible Things

Can one believe impossible things? That is the question that faces us when we approach the subject of the Trinity as revealed in the Bible. The Bible sets forth the unity of the Godhead as well as a distinctiveness of three personalities that make up the Godhead. God is one and three, an impossible concept so far as our minds can conceptualize. Yet this is a fact set forth in the Bible.

The first introduction to the plurality of God is found in Genesis 1:26, 27. "Then God said, 'Let Us make man in Our image, according to Our likeness; and let them rule over the fish of the sea and over the birds of the sky and over the cattle and over all the earth and over every creeping thing that creeps on the earth.' " You will note that this is a conversation within the Godhead. God is talking to God. The plural pronouns suggest at least two individuals are involved in the conversation.

But the next verse switches back to the singular. "And God created man in His own image, in the image of God He created him; male and female He created them" (Genesis 1:27). So in these two verses we find a marvelous revelation of the unity and plurality of the Godhead.

Another evidence of the plurality of God in these verses is found in the name *Elohim* which is translated God. This name is plural in number, indicating that there is more than one "personality" in the Godhead.

The *im* ending on a noun in the Hebrew is like the *s* ending in English. Therefore, Genesis 1:1 could read, "In the beginning Gods created the heavens and the earth." The noun is plural, but it has a singular concept. The verb that goes with it is singular.

There are many allusions to the trinitarian nature of God in both the Old and New Testaments. Isaiah 6:3 is a good example. The seraphim which Isaiah saw cried to one another, "Holy, Holy, Holy." Isaiah 48:16 is a prophetic verse spoken by Jesus in which all three members of the Godhead are put together. "And now the Lord God has sent Me, and His Spirit."

The three members of the Godhead are revealed in several passages: God the Father (1 Peter 1:2; John 6:27; Ephesians 4:6), God the Son (John 1:1; 17:5; 20:28; Titus 2:13), God the Holy Spirit (Acts 5:3, 4; 1 Corinthians 6:11; Genesis 1:2; Psalm 139:7; Romans 8:26). The concept of a triune God is impossible to comprehend and difficult to define.

## Attempting a Definition

How does one define the Trinity? Dr. B. B. Warfield has given the most concise definition and perhaps the most accurate.

The term "trinity" is not a biblical term, and we are not using biblical language when we define what is expressed by it as the doctrine that there is one only and true God, but in the unity of the Godhead there are three coeternal and coequal persons, the same in substance but distinct in subsistence.[2]

In using the term "substance," Warfield refers to God's essential nature or being, and the word "subsistence" refers to His quality of existence. The Godhead is the same in nature but distinct in existence.

However, there is a problem with the use of the word "persons" to define the Trinity. The word suggests that there are three separate rational and moral individuals in the Godhead. Such is not what the Bible reveals. The Godhead is made up of three personalities that make up one divine substance.

Many attempts have been made to give a definition to the Biblical revelation of the Godhead. The *Westminister Shorter Catechism* worded a definition this way:

Are there more Gods than one? There is but one only, the living and true God. How many persons are there in the Godhead? There are three persons in the Godhead, the Father, the Son, and the Holy Ghost; and these three are one God, the same in substance, equal in power and glory.[3]

The names that are given to God do not suggest that there is a stair-step order in the divine Godhead with the Father possessing greater power than the Son and the Son possessing a greater degree of divinity than the Spirit. The revelation of the names communicates to man how God has provided a complete scheme of redemption. God is the Father in redemption, establishing the marvelous scheme by which lawless man can be redeemed. God is the Son in redemption carrying out the sacrificial will of God in a human body in order to pay the legal penalty for sin. God is the Holy Spirit in redemption revealing the message and guiding the men who wrote it. The marvelous text in Hebrews 10:5-17 reveals how the Godhead participated in the redemption of mankind. Read it carefully and marvel at what God has done:

Therefore, when He comes into the world, He says, "Sacrifice and offering Thou hast not desired, but a body Thou hast prepared for Me; in whole burnt offerings and sacrifices for sin Thou hast taken no pleasure." Then I said, "Behold I have come (in the roll of the book it is written of Me) to do Thy will, O God." After saying above, "Sacrifices and offerings and whole burnt offerings and sacrifices for sin Thou hast not desired, nor hast Thou taken pleasure in them" (which are offered according to the Law), then He said, "Behold I have come to do Thy will." He takes away the first in order to establish the second. By this will we have been sanctified through the offering of the body of Jesus Christ once for all. And every priest stands daily ministering and offering time after time the same sacrifices, which can never take away sins; but He, having offered one sacrifice for sins for all time, sat down at the right hand of God, waiting from that time onward until His enemies be made a footstool for His feet. For by one offering He has perfected for all time those who are sanctified. And the Holy Spirit also bars witness to us; for after saying, "This is the covenant that I will make with them after those days, says the Lord: I will put My laws upon their heart, and upon their mind I will write them," He then says, "And their sins and their lawless deeds I will remember no more."

Note the revelation of the work of the Trinity in this text:

    The Father - Prepared a body for Jesus.
                 Prepared a plan -"will."
      The Son - Obeyed God's will.
                 Established a new covenant.
                 Offered His body by God's will.
                 Sanctified those who believe.
  The Holy Spirit - Bears witness through prophecy.
                 Inspired Jeremiah to prophecy
                 about the new covenant.

All three members are equal in power and glory and yet they are distinct in existence, each capable of doing a unique work distinctive from the others.

## A Witness in Nature

Just as a book reveals the mind of the author and a painting reveals the vision of the painter, even so one can expect nature to reveal something about the God behind its creation. "The heavens are telling of the glory of God; and their expanse is declaring the work of His hands" (Psalm 19:1). In the book of Romans, the apostle Paul declares that God's divine nature (Theiotes = divinity or Godhead, having to do with His nature) is revealed in nature. "For since the creation of the world His invisible attributes, His eternal power and divine nature, have been clearly seen, being understood through what has been made, so that they are without excuse" (Romans 1:20).

The very first verse of the Bible begins with a revelation of the tri-unity of creation. "In the beginning (time), God created the heaven (space) and the earth (matter)" (Genesis 1:1). The very nature or "structure" of God's existence is thus revealed in creation.

What is even more remarkable is that the three components of nature each has a tri-unity. Space has three dimensions: length, width, height. Time also is a trinity: past, present, future. Matter is composed of energy, motion, and phenomena. The divine nature and the phenomenon of creation are illustrated in figure 2.

Many illustrations in nature reveal a tri-unity existence. Water, for example, retains its chemical identity whether in solid, gas, or liquid state. It is possible for water to co-exist in equilibrium as ice, steam, and liquid, provided it has the proper temperature and pressure. Nevertheless, we would not say that water is like the Godhead. It reveals clearly the eternal power and divine nature of the One who made it.

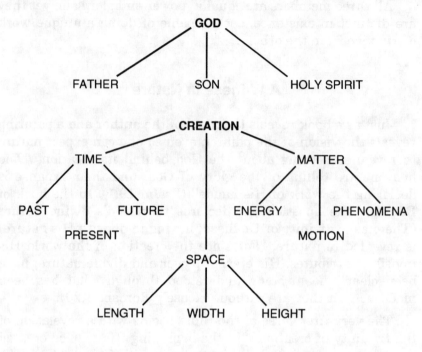

*Figure No. 2*

## Uniqueness of the Trinity

The revelation of the Trinity in Scripture is absolutely unique. Other religions have their gods, but nowhere is there found the unusual concept of a triune God as is revealed in the Bible. This is one evidence of the Bible's divine origin. If men had written the Bible on their own initiative, without divine guidance, they would not have presented concepts that are impossible to comprehend and so difficult to define. It is only logical that if human minds dreamed up the idea of the Trinity, there would have been some explanation of its meaning and existence. Yet the Bible sets forth the concept as truth with no effort made on the part of the writers to explain its meaning.

Because the Trinity is a difficult concept to grasp, many religions have gone to extremes in trying to deal with the antinomy. For example, in *The Kingdom Interlinear Translation of the Greek Scriptures*, the translators render John 1:1 in this manner: "In the beginning the Word was, and the Word was with God, and the Word was a god."[4] A footnote on the word "god" reads: "A god in contrast with the God." In other words, the Word, who is Jesus Christ, was a divine being but not a part of God Himself. This, of course, is a perversion of the text that should read: "In the beginning was the Word, and the Word was with God, and the Word was God" (N.A.S.V.).

## Dealing With the Antinomy

What choices do we have when we are faced with an antinomy in Scripture? One would be to try to reduce it to the level of human understanding. Another would be to deny it as impossible to believe. A third choice would be to accept both parts of the revelation as truth.

This choice requires faith in the revelation, but it is a faith that is built on solid evidence that the concept is a true presentation of the unknown facts. Such a faith will prevent one from going off in directions that are misleading and erroneous. Accepting the concept of the Trinity as truth lays a good foundation for the other antinomies that will be encountered throughout the Bible.

## Notes

[1] Lewis Carroll, *The Annotated Alice* (New York: Clarkson N. Potter, 1960), p. 251.

[2] B. B. Warfield, "Trinity," in James Orr (ed.), *The International Standard Bible Encylcopedia* (Grand Rapids, MI: Wm. B. Eerdmans Publishing Co., 1939), Vol. V, p. 3012.

[3] James Oliver Buswell Jr., "Trinity," *Zondervan Pictorial Bible Dictionary* (Grand Rapids, MI: Zondervan Publishing House, 1963), p. 871.

⁴New World Translation Committee, *The Kingdom Interlinear Translation of the Greek Scripture* (Brooklyn: Watchtower Bible and Tract Society of New York, 1969), p. 417.

## Remembering the Facts

1. How is the plurality of God revealed in Genesis 1:26, 27?

2. Why is the name "Elohim" significant in relationship to the Godhead?

3. Hebrews 10:5-17 reveals the various works of the Trinity. List one significant work for each:

   The Father-

   The Son -

   The Holy Spirit -

4. How does Genesis 1:1 reveal the tri-unity of creation?

5. Give some examples of how God's nature is revealed in creation.

6. How is the revelation of the trinity evidence of the Bible's divine origin?

7. Give an example of how the Jehovah's Witnesses' translation goes to an extreme in dealing with the antinomy of the Godhead.

8. List the three choices we have when faced with an antinomy in Scripture:

    (1)


    (2)


    (3)


9. What is the best choice? What is required to make it?


10. When our faith is strong enough to deal with the antinomy, what danger will we avoid?


## Discussing the Issues

1. Why is it so difficult to think of God the Father, the Son, and the Holy Spirit as being equal in all respects?


2. How does the triune nature of God affect our worship? Do you find it difficult to center your worship upon the person of God? Why?


3. Why do you think the Holy Spirit has become so prominent in our day among so many religious groups?


4. Is it possible to overemphasize the work of one member of the Godhead? How? What possible damage could that produce?

# Chapter 3
# Jesus Christ—God or Man?

> . . . and the Holy Spirit descended upon Him in bodily form like a dove, and a voice came out of heaven, "Thou art *My beloved Son*, in Thee I am well pleased" (Luke 3:22; emphasis added).

> For the *Son of Man* has come to seek and to save that which was lost (Luke 19:10; emphasis added).

There is a difference between an antinomy and a paradox. A paradox can be defined as an apparent contradiction. With additional thought and investigation, a paradox usually can be reconciled. The antinomy contains truths that in most cases cannot be reconciled.

The biblical revelation of Jesus Christ contains an antinomy because Jesus is presented in Scripture as the Son of God and the Son of Man. The antinomy lies in the fact that divinity and humanity are not the same.

In the introduction of this book I presented some of the opinions that people have held concerning the incarnation of Jesus Christ. In the year A.D. 451 the Chalcedonian Definition was drawn up which stated that Christ was both God and man, "Perfect in divinity, perfect in humanity; truly God and truly man." This definition states that Jesus was both human and divine. That concept is the core of the Christian faith.

The apostle Paul set forth this fact very clearly. "For it was the Father's good pleasure for all the fullness to dwell in Him, and through Him to reconcile all things to Himself, having made peace through the blood of His cross; through Him, I say, whether things on earth or in heaven" (Colossians 1:19, 20).

The very basis of our redemption is found in the deity/humanity of Jesus Christ. Without a proper understanding of the incarnation, we are left with no certain explanation of how salvation is accomplished. Paul makes it clear that the fullness of God has its permanent location in Jesus. In Jesus God was present in the world reconciling lost humanity to Himself.

## The Son of God

It was well known in Jewish theology during the time of Christ that the Messiah would be known as the Son of God. This is true because Psalm 2:7 declared that the Messiah would be God's Son. "I will surely tell of the decree of the Lord. He said to me, 'Thou art my Son, Today I have begotten Thee.' " On three different occasions during the life of Christ God declared the Sonship of Christ with a verbal announcement from heaven (Matthew 3:17; 17:5; John 12:27-30).

When God acknowledged that Jesus was His Son, He was not referring to Jesus' origin as line of descent. The Scriptures teach Jesus did not descend from God the Father nor was He generated by or originated from Him, but rather Jesus was an eternal being.

The significance of the Father-Son relationship between God and Jesus is one of essence. Jesus and God are of the same nature. The title "Son of God" refers to Jesus' nature and characteristics. When Jesus referred to God as His Father, He was claiming an equality with God because they both possessed the same nature or essence. This, in fact, is exactly how the Jews understood the expression, as we shall see later.

It is important to understand that Jesus did not claim to be *a* son of God but *the* Son of God in a unique sense. "All things have been handed over to Me by My Father; and no one knows the Son, except the Father; nor does anyone know the Father, except the Son, and anyone to whom the Son wills to reveal Him" (Matthew 11:27). This is a remarkable statement because Jesus claims a special, unique relationship with God the Father, shared by no one else. This no doubt went a step beyond what the Jews expected to hear even from the Messiah.

When it dawned upon His listeners that Jesus was revealing His divine nature through the term "Son of God," they became enraged. John reveals their reaction. "But He answered them, 'My Father is working until now, and I Myself am working.' For this cause therefore the Jews were seeking all the more to kill Him, because He not only was breaking the Sabbath, but also was calling God His own Father, making Himself equal with God" (John 5:17, 18).

The following verses in John 5 are astounding. Instead of shrinking back from His accusers, Jesus becomes even more bold in revealing His deity.

*Equal With God in Working.* "Jesus therefore answered and was saying to them, 'Truly, truly, I say to you, the Son can do nothing of Himself, unless it is something He sees the Father doing; for whatever the Father does, these things the Son also does in like manner' " (verse 19).

*Equal With God in Knowledge.* "For the Father loves the Son, and shows Him all things that He Himself is doing; and greater works than these will He show Him, that you may marvel" (verse 20).

*Equal With God in Life-Giving Power.* "For just as the Father raises the dead and gives them life, even so the Son also gives life to whom He wishes" (verse 21).

*Equal With God in Honor.* "For not even the Father judges anyone, but He has given all judgment to the Son, in order that all may honor the Son, even as they honor the Father. He who does not honor the Son does not honor the Father who sent Him" (verses 22, 23).

*Equal With God in Regeneration.* "Truly, truly, I say to you, he who hears My word, and believes Him who sent Me, has eternal life, and does not come into judgment, but has passed out of death into life. Truly, truly, I say to you, an hour is coming and now is, when the dead shall hear the voice of the Son of God; and those who hear shall live" (verses 24, 25).

*Equal With God in Self-Existence.* " For just as the Father has life in Himself, even so He gave to the Son also to have life in Himself" (verse 26).

*Equal With God in Judging.* "And He gave Him authority to execute judgment, because He is the Son of Man" (verse 27).

*Equal With God in Resurrection Power.* "Do not marvel at this; for an hour is coming, in which all who are in the tombs shall hear His voice, and shall come forth; those who did the good deeds to a resurrection of life, those who committed the evil deeds to a resurrection of judgment" (verses 28, 29).

If these claims were not enough, on one occasion Jesus identified Himself as the God of the Old Testament. In John 8:58 He said, "Truly, truly, I say to you, before Abraham was born, I Am." In Exodus 3:14, God revealed Himself to Moses as "I Am." No less than twenty-three times John records the Lord's use of the name "I Am," identifying Himself as the God of history recorded in the Old Testament. John records the seven great "I Am's" of Jesus, each followed by a great metaphor revealing His work of redemption:

> "I Am the Bread of Life" (6:35, 41, 48, 51).
> "I Am the Light of the World" (8:12).
> "I Am the Door of the Sheep" (10:7, 9).
> "I Am the Good Shepherd" (10:11, 14).
> "I Am the Resurrection and the Life" (11:25).
> "I Am the Way, the Truth, the Life" (14:6).
> "I Am the True Vine" (15:1, 5).

John also recorded seven miracles, each of which reveals a different aspect of Christ's divinity.

| | | |
|---|---|---|
| John 2:1-11 | Water to wine | Master of quality |
| John 4:43-54 | Healing of the nobleman's son 20 miles away | Master of distance |
| John 5:1-14 | Healing of man crippled for 38 years | Master of time |

| | | |
|---|---|---|
| John 6:1-14 | Miraculous feeding 5,000 people | Master of quantity |
| John 6:16-24 | Walked on water | Master of natural law |
| John 9:1-38 | Healing of man born blind | Master over misfortune |
| John 11:1-44 | Raising of Lazarus from the dead | Master over death[1] |

John concluded his account of Jesus' life with these words: "Many other signs therefore Jesus also performed in the presence of the disciples which are not written in this book; but these have been written that you may believe that Jesus is the Christ, the Son of God; and that believing you may have life in His name" (John 20:30, 31).

A proper understanding and belief in Jesus as God's Son is absolutely essential in order to possess eternal life. However, it is important to recognize that Jesus was not only 100 percent God, but He was also 100 percent man, as well.

## The Son of Man

Jesus was not a phantom, as the Gnostics believed, but rather He was a real person, possessing a flesh-and-blood body. The apostle John began his account of the incarnation by describing Christ in eternity and then showing His entry into His own creation. Dr. J. I. Packer has given an excellent summary of John 1:1-14.

1. *"In the beginning was the word"* (verse 1). Here is the Word's eternity. He had no beginning of His own, when other things began, He—was.

2. *"And the Word was with God"* (verse 1). Here is the Word's personality. The power that fulfills God's purposes is the power of a distinct personal being, who stands in an eternal relation to God of active fellowship (this is what the phrase means).

3. *"And the Word was God"* (verse 1). Here is the Word's deity. Though personally distinct from the Father, He is not a creature; He is divine in Himself, as the Father is. The mystery with which this verse confronts us is thus the mystery of personal distinctions within the unity of the Godhead.

4. *"All things were made by Him"* (verse 3). Here is the Word creating. He was the Father's agent in every act of making that the Father has ever performed. All that was made was made through Him. (Here, incidentally, is further proof that He, the Maker, does not belong to the class of things made, any more than the Father does.

5. *"In Him was life"* (verse 4). Here is the Word animating. There is no physical life in the realm of created things save in and through Him. Here is the Bible answer to the problem of the origin and continuance of life, in all its forms: life is given and maintained by the Word. Created things do not have life in themselves, but life in the Word, the second person of the Godhead.

6. *"And the life was the light of men"* (verse 4). Here is the Word revealing. In giving life, He gives light too; that is to say, every man receives intimations of God from the very fact of his being alive in God's world, and this, no less than the fact that he is alive, is due to the work of the Word.

7. *"And the Word became flesh"* (verse 14). Here is the Word incarnate. The baby in the manger at Bethlehem was none other than the eternal Word of God.[2]

The apostle Paul also developed the divinity/humanity of Christ in a similar fashion.

> Have this attitude in yourselves which was also in Christ Jesus, who, although He existed in the form of God, did not regard equality with God a thing to be grasped, but emptied Himself, taking the form of a bond-servant, and being made in the likeness of men. And being found in appearance as a man, he humbled Himself by becoming obedient to the point of death, even death on a cross. Therefore, God highly exalted Him, and bestowed on Him the name

which is above every name, that at the name of Jesus every knee should bow, of those who are in heaven, and on earth, and under the earth, and that every tongue should confess that Jesus Christ is Lord, to the glory of God the Father (Philippians 2:5-11).

Figure 3 is a visual outline of Paul's revelation of Christ's pilgrimage into the world that He created.

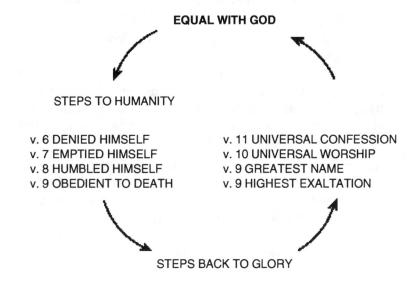

**EQUAL WITH GOD**

STEPS TO HUMANITY

| | |
|---|---|
| v. 6 DENIED HIMSELF | v. 11 UNIVERSAL CONFESSION |
| v. 7 EMPTIED HIMSELF | v. 10 UNIVERSAL WORSHIP |
| v. 8 HUMBLED HIMSELF | v. 9 GREATEST NAME |
| v. 9 OBEDIENT TO DEATH | v. 9 HIGHEST EXALTATION |

STEPS BACK TO GLORY

*Figure No. 3*

The question arises: Did Christ surrender His deity in becoming a man? The answer is found in the Greek word "Kenoo," which is translated "emptied" (verse 7). The Greek scholar W. E. Vine observes, "Christ did not empty Himself of Godhood. He did not cease to be what He essentially and eternally was."[3] So we can say that He remained what He was and became what we are. It is easy to say but difficult to comprehend!

Logic would dictate that if Jesus was God in the beginning, it would not be possible for Him to become anything less than God at any time. But the question still remains: How did Christ empty Himself? The answer must lie in His attitude of humility which Paul is developing. Christ was willing to relinquish His glory, that is, the use of His divine attributes. His glory was veiled with human flesh just as a bright light may be veiled with a filter. The filter does not diminish the brightness of the light, it only limits the extent to which the light can be used. Just so, the human body that Jesus possessed was a kind of veil that limited Jesus' glory only so far as man was concerned. His divine attributes were always present, but only occasionally were they brought to full potential while He was on earth (e.g., The Mount of Transfiguration, Matthew 17, Mark 9, Luke 9).

Jesus chose to limit His divinity with the "appearance as a man." At any given moment He possessed the ability to utilize His divine powers. When He chose to do so, a revelation of His deity was given to man. The writers of the gospels (Matthew, Mark, Luke, and John) recorded those instances of divine glory in order that we may know that Jesus was indeed God in the flesh.

The record also tells us that He was human. He became tired, hungry, and depressed. The Hebrew writer described His humanity with these words: "In the days of His flesh, He offered up both prayers and supplications with loud crying and tears to the One able to save Him from death, and He was heard because of His piety. Although He was a Son, He learned obedience from the things which He suffered" (Hebrews 5:7, 8). Note the words in these verses that refer to His humanity—flesh, prayers, supplications, crying, tears, obedience, and suffered. The Hebrew writer concluded, "Although He was a Son, He learned obedience. . . ." To say it another way, "Although He was God, He limited His divine attributes and learned how to obey just like any other human being."

## More Than a Myth

With the antinomy of the God/Man before us, we are faced with the question: Is this a myth? When we think of myths, there are certain ones that come to mind, such as the Greek Thesus, the Egyptian Isis and Osiris, the Thor and Odin of the Scandinavian legends, the Hindustance Vishnu, Buddha, and scores of others that have come from poetry, traditions, superstitions, and religions of other nations.

Mythological gods are usually related to various events in nature. For example, the people of Java have a legend concerning the eclipses of the sun. They believe that when an eclipse occurs the sun is swallowed by the severed head of the evil giant Kala Rau, who was beheaded trying to drink a magic potion of the gods. His body fell to earth and became the "lesung," a concave vessel in which rice is pounded to be hulled.

So during an eclipse of the sun the Javanese beat on the giant's body—their "lesungs"—to make the head let go of the sun. Obviously, it always works.

An outstanding book by Atticus G. Haygood entitled *The Man of Galiee*[4] presents the following reasons why Jesus Christ cannot be counted among the myths of history:

1. Myths originate and, as conceptions, are complete before written history.
2. About all myths there is something grotesque if not monstrous.
3. Myths reflect their time, place, and race.
4. In all nations myths defy chronology; they are without dates.
5. Myths defy topography as they do chronology; they are not only without dates, they are without definite localities.
6. Myths are not completed at once. They require a long time— ages—for their development.
7. All myths belong to the infancy, never to the age of any nation. They spring out of the morning mists; they never appear in the light of day.

It is obvious that the story of Jesus Christ does not fit the pattern of myths. We are, therefore, left with one conclusion— Jesus Christ was a real person of history. The revelation of Him in the Bible is true . . . Jesus was God in the flesh.

The marvelous love that prompted Christ to relinquish the use of His divine attributes, enter human flesh, suffer, and die on the cross is beyond our ability to understand. We can only marvel that God would go to such great lengths to recover His creation that had rebelled against His holy will. We must stand in awe of the great revelation in God's Word concerning Jesus, the Messiah, the only begotten Son of God.

## Worshiping the Son

In that marvelous text we have just studied (John 5), Jesus said, "He who does not honor the Son does not honor the Father who sent Him" (verse 23). The word "honor" implies worship. This verse has important implications in the way we direct our worship. When Thomas fell on his knees before the Lord, he said, "My Lord and my God!" (John 20:28). Thomas was fulfilling the proper perspective of worship because God can only be worshiped as He is perceived through Jesus Christ. When we worship Jesus as God through our singing, praying, teaching, giving, and communion, we are in fact honoring God. Worship of the Father cannot be separated from worship of the Son.

God is revealed in Scripture as the Father of the Lord Jesus Christ, not some vague, undefined spirit being. When we understand that God is of the same nature and essence as Jesus, we can properly direct our praise to Him. Jesus said, "No one comes to the Father, but through Me" (John 14:6). What great honor we have as rebels against God, to draw near in repentance and faith in Christ and worship God in spirit and in truth!

## Notes

[1]Gene A. Getz, *Loving One Another* (Wheaton, IL: Victor Books, 1979), pp. 50-51.

[2]J. I. Packer, *Knowing God* (Downers Grove, IL: Inter Varsity Press, 1973), pp. 48-49.

[3]W. E. Vine, *An Expository Dictionary of New Testament Words* (Old Tappan, NJ: Fleming H. Revell Co., 1940), Vol. 2, p. 25.

[4]Atticus G. Haygood, *The Man of Galilee* (Nashville, TN: M.E. Church, 1889), pp. 43-49.

## Remembering the Facts

1. What is the difference between an antinomy and a paradox?


2. Why is the revelation of Jesus as the Son of God and the Son of Man an antinomy?


3. What passage of Scripture in the Old Testament declared that the Messiah would be the Son of God?


4. What did the Jews understand the term "Son of God" to mean?


5. In John 5 there are eight areas in which Jesus is equal with God. List them:

   (1)


   (2)


   (3)


   (4)


   (5)


   (6)

(7)


(8)


6. Philippians 2:5-11 reveals the divinity/humanity of Jesus, demonstrating His equality with God and His identity with man. List the steps:

Steps to Humanity:

Steps to Glory:

7. In what way did Jesus "empty Himself" when He became a man?


8. What are some of the human characteristics of Jesus revealed in Hebrews 5:7, 8?


9. There are seven identifying characteristics of myths. How does Jesus Christ defy each one?
Prehistorical-


Grotesque-


Reflection of time/place/race-


Chronology-


Topography-

Longevity of development-

Infancy beginning-

## Discussing the Issues

1.  Why do you think it was necessary for God (Jesus) to become a man (fully human)?

2.  Do you believe Jesus dealt with His temptations from the strength of His divinity or from the strength of His humanity? Or from both?

3.  What significance does the divinity/humanity of Jesus have in regard to His atoning death on the cross?

4.  What is the proper view of Jesus that each Christian should hold while praying to God through Jesus' name? Should Jesus be thought of as equal with God or subordinate to God?

# Chapter 4
# Creation—Good or Evil?

And God saw all that He had made, and behold, it was very good (Genesis 1:31).

For we know that the whole creation groans and suffers the pains of childbirth together until now (Romans 8:22).

The Bible declares that when God finished His act of creation, He surveyed all that He had made and pronounced it "very good." Since God is the absolute standard of goodness, we would conclude that out of an infinity of possible worlds which God could have created, the one He chose was the very best. The world God created contained the greatest amount of good that was possible.

If this is true, then why is there so much suffering and evil in our world? Destruction and misery are omnipresent. Since all things have their origin with God, the question arises—isn't God to blame for all that happens in the world, including the pain and sin?

In his treatise on the Wrath of God, Lactantius quoted Epicurus' statement of logic concerning the problem of evil as follows:

God either wishes to take away evils and is unable; or he is able and unwilling; or he is neither willing nor able, or he is both willing and able. If he is willing and unable, he is feeble, which is not in accordance with the character of god; if he is able and not willing, he is envious, which is equally at variance with god; if he is neither willing nor able, he is both envious and feeble, and therefore, not god; if he is both willing and able, which is alone suitable to god, from what source then are evils? Or why does he not remove them?[1]

Bertrand Russell rejected Christ as Savior because He knew how to heal and relieve humanity of its pain and miseries, but refused to do so.

Here we find another antinomy because the Bible clearly teaches that God is good, kind, and benevolent, yet it also acknowledges that evil exists in the world.

## The Problem With Good

The problem of evil really stems from a definition of what is good. The atheist argues against God's existence on the basis of a certain definition of good and evil. But the real question is: Why does the atheist hate evil, pain, and suffering so much? How does one justify that hatred? C. S. Lewis argues this point convincingly:

> Unless we take our own standard of goodness to be valid in principle (however fallible our particular applications of it) we cannot mean anything by calling waste and cruelty evils. And unless we take our own standard to be something more than ours, to be in fact an objective principle to which we are responding, we cannot regard that standard as valid. In a word, unless we allow ultimate reality to be moral, we cannot morally condemn it.[2]

Lewis has made a valid point. The fact that man defines something as good or evil says that there must be a standard outside himself. Where does man find his definition of good?

Let's suppose a visitor from outer space comes to the earth and observes life on this planet with all its evils, sickness, sufferings, and death. He could read in the newspapers about war and crime on a daily basis. The visitor would discover man's inhumanity; he would learn of violent earthquakes, floods, and tornadoes.

If someone told the visitor that there was a sovereign God who loves man and is concerned for his welfare, the visitor would be very surprised to learn of man's belief in such a God. And his surprise would be understandable. He would want to know where in all the universe did man get the idea that there is a loving, benevolent God?

The point is, if there were not such a God, it is unlikely human beings would have invented Him. The only way man can define what is good is by its relationship with an ultimate standard of goodness, which is God. The hatred of pain and suffering and other forms of evil are man's expression of a desire for goodness. That desire comes from God's revelation of Himself as a kind, loving Creator. The fact that even an atheist can define good and evil tells us there are ultimate moral issues in the world.

Now the atheist cannot have it both ways. If there is not an ultimate standard of goodness, then evil is not morally evil. If that is the case, then to argue that the world of suffering and death is a reflection on a good God is empty rhetoric.

On the other hand, if God is the standard of goodness, then it is His responsibility to show how pain and evil can be beneficial. That being the case, man will have to allow for God's definition to suffice even in those cases where pain and suffering will seem to be meaningless, insofar as man is able to discern.

## The Origin of Evil

Creation in its original condition met God's approval. It was a true reflection of the God who made it. As He progressed through His work of creation, God continually analyzed His work.

> And God saw that the light was good (Genesis 1:4).

> And God called the dry land earth, and the gathering of the waters He called seas; and God saw that it was good (Genesis 1:10).

> And the earth brought forth vegetation, plants yielding seed after their kind and trees bearing fruit, with seed in them, after their kind; and God saw that it was good (Genesis 1:12).

> And God made the two great lights, the greater light to govern the day, and the lesser light to govern the night. He made the stars also. And God placed them in the expanse of the heavens to give light on the earth, and to govern the day and the night, and to separate the light from the darkness; and God saw that it was good (Genesis 1:16-18).
>
> And God created the great sea monsters, and every living creature that moves, with which the waters swarmed after their kind, and every winged bird after its kind; and God saw that it was good (Genesis 1:21).
>
> And God made the beasts of the earth after their kind, and the cattle after their kind, and everything that creeps on the ground after its kind; and God saw that it was good (Genesis 1:25).
>
> And God saw all that He had made, and behold, it was very good (Genesis 1:31).

It is important to realize that God made a world that was good in every respect. Every step of creation, according to the judgment of God, was good, and the combination of all His created works was "very good." At the conclusion of God's acts of creation, there was no sin, no evil—only total goodness. That is creation functioning as God approves it and desires it to be. It is a creation that reflects the glory of His goodness.

Man was the final product of God's creation and the highest order of all creatures. The uniqueness of man's creation is seen in the fact that he was made in the "image of God"(Genesis 1:26, 27). What does that mean? Some have thought it refers to his power of speech, others say it is his ability to reason and think. Still others believe it refers to man's moral values. Some see it as man's ability to believe in God. Karl Barth saw it as the potential for interpersonal relationships of which male and female is a prototype.

Since the Bible does not give us a precise definition of the meaning of the "image of God," we must be careful in drawing a dogmatic conclusion as to its meaning. Perhaps all of the above definitions are a part of the meaning. There is one word that seems to sum up the meaning of the "image of God," and that word is freedom. Man was created with freedom or the capacity to choose. "And the Lord God commanded the man saying, 'From any tree of the garden you may eat freely; but from the tree of the knowledge of good and evil you shall not eat, for in the day that you eat from it you shall surely die'" (Genesis 2:16, 17).

It is obvious from the reading of Genesis 1 and 2 that man was created with the freedom to choose to believe or disbelieve, obey or disobey, love or hate. Inherent in the freedom to choose is the possibility of evil. To say that God has the ability to create a world free from pain and evil does not answer the question concerning the existence of evil. Surely God can create such a world, but what kind of world would it be? One fact is sure, there could not be freedom in such a world, because a creature that has freedom to choose love must also have equal freedom to choose hate; otherwise, freedom would not exist.

In the Bible we find man, the pinnacle of creation, bearing the very image of his Creator, free to choose the course and direction of his life. I like the term Dr. Francis Schaeffer used, a free man with an "unprogrammed choice."[3] That means that God allowed man the freedom to determine his own destiny. Apparently God also created angels with the same kind of freedom (see Ezekiel 28 and Revelation 12). Isaiah 14:12-15 has a primary reference to the monarch of Babylon; however, some scholars have seen a symbolic reference here to Satan's pride and fall. Just as the king defied God and desired to rule over the utmost limits of the earth ("the north" vs. 13), Satan was also lifted up with pride and desired to rule above God Himself!

The text reads:

> How you have fallen from heaven, O star of the morning, son of the dawn! You have been cut down to the earth, you who have weakened the nations! But you said in your heart, "I will ascend to heaven; I will raise my throne above the stars of God, and I will sit on the mount of assembly in the recesses of the north. I will ascend above the heights of the clouds; I will make myself like the Most High."

Nevertheless you will be thrust down to Sheol, to the recesses of the pit.

The phrase "star of the morning" is from the Hebrew word "Helel," which means "shining one" (Lucifer, K.J.V.). The language here is similar to that which is used in the New Testament to describe Satan's fall (Luke 10:18; Revelation 12:8, 9). The point is that the king of Babylon chose to rebel and lifted himself above God, which is symbolic of Satan's choice to lift himself above the Most High. When the serpent (Satan) approached Eve, the scripture says, "And the serpent said to the woman, 'You surely shall not die! For God knows that in the day you eat from it your eyes will be opened, and you will be like God, knowing good and evil' " (Genesis 3:4, 5). Eve chose to rebel! Therefore, sin, suffering, and sorrow entered God's created order.

A revolt had started in heaven, perhaps sometime after the creation of the world. Soon afterward, Satan brought an outside temptation to man. Man chose to disbelieve God and disobey His command. Then sin, evil, pain, and death entered God's creation (read Genesis 3:14-19, Romans 8:18-23, Revelation 22:3). The choice that man made resulted in alienation from God. Before long man chose to hate and kill (Genesis 3). Thus the freedom to choose resulted in much misery, heartache, and physical suffering.

However, we must understand that God desired a much different world for man. Sin, sickness, and death are a part of God's permissive will, not His perfect will.

## God's Foreknowledge

Did God know that man would sin? The answer is yes. God, knowing man would revolt, planned for his redemption before the "foundations of the world" (Ephesians 1:4; 1 Peter 1:20; Revelation 13:8; 17:8). But why would God create man in the first place if He knew that man would suffer as a result of sin? Wouldn't a loving God choose not to create a world of sin? Wouldn't the eternal death of one person be too much for a loving

God to endure? Why didn't He just drop the plan of creation if He knew that it would not meet His approval?

The answer to these questions lies in the depth of God's eternal love. Dr. A. E. Wilder-Smith illustrates the dilemma beautifully:

> On the very day of our wedding, we know that one day the pain of separation from our partner through death is inevitable. We accept this future loss of joy because we believe that the present ennoblement of character in giving ourselves to the other in love even for just a single day is better than no love at all. In marrying, we accept the utter misery of certain separation and death as the end of marriage, because we believe that one day of love and joy is worth more than the ultimate separation and misery at the end of marriage.
>
> Evidently, God also feels this way, because in order to have the possibility of some love, joy, and virtue, He accepted the accompanying certainty of hate and vice. It is a question of balance. Those who have known love will admit that it weighs infinitely more than the distress which its freedom may bring with it. Apparently, the Creator, the God of love, agrees—for He went ahead with our creation in spite of the foreseeable mess which would result. He was convinced that the warmth of true love is worth infinitely more than the bitterness of suffering. Where life is, the opportunity to love exists, too.
>
> We shall escape the trials and sufferings of this life at death, but our character of love (ennobled through our trials) will continue to live forever. So whichever way we look, we must admit that the creation, if it produced the possibility of love, is quite worthwhile, even if suffering may be involved. For love is the greatest of all virtues and far surpasses the misery which the freedom to love may entail.[4]

So here is the antinomy—God is good. He created a good world with the possibility of evil, pain, and suffering. In His perfect foreknowledge, He saw man's rebellion and the evil results. The creation that presently exists is a fulfillment of God's loving will, even in light of the evil, pain, and death that exist in it. Although we may not be able to explain how a certain evil can fulfill God's will (e.g., Hitler's reign of terror); nevertheless, with the "eye of faith" we can believe that a good God will bring a blessing out of the tragedy.

Everything we see (both good and evil) is a fulfillment of God's ultimate purpose in creation. "The One forming light and creating darkness, causing well-being and creating calamity; I am the Lord who *does all these*" (Isaiah 45:7; emphasis added).

When we look at the cross and the love of God displayed in the giving of Christ for the redemption of man, we must admit that even the sin that brought about such a deed resulted in good. For without the sin of Adam we would never know the love of Christ in His atonement. The great, omnipotent God can make even the wrath of man praise Him (Psalm 76:10).

> Oh, the depth of the riches both of the wisdom and knowledge of God! How unsearchable are His judgments and unfathomable His ways! For who has known the mind of the Lord, or who became His counselor? Or who has first given to Him that it might be paid back to Him again? For from Him and through Him and to Him are all things. To Him be the glory forever. Amen (Romans 11:33-36).

## Our Response

God chose the very best plan for creation. It is a plan that reveals His power and glory. The suffering and death of Christ display the wisdom and beauty of God's love. "Worthy is the Lamb that was slain to receive power and riches and wisdom and might and honor and glory and blessing" (Revelation 5:12). The creation as it stands today is the best of all possible creations because through the good and evil that exist, God receives the glory. No other creation could bring God the glory and honor through Christ's redemption as the one that now exists.

As we live within the confines of this creation, we, too, will experience good and evil. What should our response be?

1. First, we must realize that suffering has a meaning (1 Peter 2:20, 21; 4:1).
2. Second, we should realize it will be only temporary (Romans 8:18).
3. Third, we should expect some suffering (1 Peter 4:12-14).
4. Finally, we should rejoice that God will turn it into good (Romans 8:28).

There may be many questions still unanswered concerning the problem of evil. Each individual case of suffering poses its own particular set of questions; however, one thing is certain— God is in control and His will is being accomplished in every area. As the old Puritan Thomas Watson used to say, "Where reason cannot wade, there faith must swim."

## Notes

[1]Lactantius, "A Treatise on the Anger of God," in Alexander Roberts and James Donalson (eds.), *The Ante-Nicene Fathers, VII* (Grand Rapids, MI: Wm. B. Eerdmans Publishing Co., 1951), p. 271.

[2]C. S. Lewis, "De Futilitate," in Walter Hooper (ed.), *Christian Reflection* (Grand Rapids, MI: Wm. B. Eerdmans Publishing Co., 1967), pp. 69-70.

[3]Francis A. Schaeffer, *Genesis in Space and Time* (Downers Grove, IL: Inter Varsity Press, 1972), p. 78.

[4]A. E. Wilder-Smith, *Why Does God Allow It?!* (San Diego: Master Books, 1980), pp. 52-53.

## Remembering the Facts

1. Out of the infinite choices which God had for creation, why did He choose to create this world?

2. Why does the problem of evil stem from a definition of what is good?

3. Where does man ultimately receive his definition of "good"?

4. What fact does the atheist reveal when he argues that suffering, pain, etc., are bad?

5. As God progressed through the various stages of creation, what was His analysis of His work?

6. Why is man unique?

7. Man was created in the "image of God." What is a possible explanation of the meaning of that term?

8. Sin, sickness, and death are a part of God's permissive will, but not His p_____ will.

9. Since God foreknew that man would sin and suffer, why would He create man in the first place?

10. List the four responses that will help us cope with the evil in our lives:

    (1 )

(2)

(3)

(4)

## Discussing the Issues

1. Why is it difficult to accept suffering as a part of God's plan for our lives?

2. What outlook should a Christian take toward creation with all its pains and pleasures?

3. In view of the biblical revelation concerning God's purpose in suffering, how should the Christian pray about his own suffering?

4. Do you believe the book of Job deals with the meaning of suffering or the fact that God should be honored even when suffering is meaningless?

# Chapter 5
# The Bible—From God or Man?

All Scripture is inspired by God and is profitable for teaching, for reproof, for correction, for training in righteousness; . . . (2 Timothy 3:16).

A wife is bound as long as her husband lives; but if her husband is dead, she is free to be married to whom she wishes, only in the Lord. But *in my opinion* she is happier if she remains as she is; and *I think I also have the Spirit of God* (1 Corinthians 7:39, 40; emphasis added).

The Bible's impact on the United States is phenomenal. Americans spend millions for Bibles and each year the Gideons distribute thousands free to hotels, motels, and hospitals. It remains a best seller even though it is one of the oldest books in the world.

Our English word "Bible" came to us by way of the French language from the Latin *biblia* and the Greek *biblos*. The word dates back to the eleventh century B.C. where it referred to the outer coat of a papyrus reed.

The Bible is divided into two major parts, the Old Testament and the New Testament. The word "testament" means literally a covenant or agreement between two parties. The Old Covenant refers to the contract between God and Israel; the New Covenant refers to the new contract between God and Christians.

The outstanding feature of the Bible is its unity. The one theme developed from Genesis to Revelation is the *Messiah*.

The Old Testament prophecied His coming; the New Testament revealed His person and presence during a certain time in history. Augustine said the New Testament is veiled in the Old

Testament and the Old Testament is unveiled in the New Testament. To say it another way, Christ is enfolded in the Old Testament, but unfolded in the New.

## The Mystery

The great mystery surrounding the Bible is its origin. It claims a divine origin and a human origin. It was inspired by God and written by men. Like Jesus Christ, the Bible is completely divine and completely human as well.

The antinomy which the Bible presents has produced various approaches to Scripture. Thomas Jefferson did not believe the Bible was divinely inspired. With scissors and paste in hand, Jefferson sat down with a Bible and began cutting verse by verse and arranging the verses in a manner coinciding with his own point of view.

The result of this effort was a forty-six-page book entitled *The Life and Morals of Jesus of Nazareth*. The amazing thing about Jefferson's effort is that he was able to accomplish this feat in one or two nights while he was serving as President of the United States.

Another example of the various views people take concerning the Bible is that of Rudolf Bultmann. Bultmann believed the Bible contains a great deal of "meat and milk, but also a great deal of sand and gravel." In other words, some elements are divine in origin and others are human in origin. In his book *Demythologizing the Bible*, Bultmann endeavored to identify truth and eliminate what he thought was myth.

So we are faced with the question: What should we believe about the Bible? Is it from God or was it produced solely by man?

## Theories of Inspiration

In 2 Timothy 3:16a it says, "All Scripture is inspired by God. . . ." The Greek word that is here translated "inspired" is *theopneustos*, which means "God-breathed," or "breathed out from God." Dr. J. I. Packer wrote, "The thought here is that, just as God made the host of heaven 'by the breath of His mouth' (Ps. 33:6), through His own creative fiat, so we should regard the scriptures as the product of a similar creative fiat."[1]

There are several theories as to how God breathed His Word into existence.

*The Mechanical or Dictation Theory*. According to this view God literally dictated the Bible and the writers were stenographers.

*The Concept of Dynamic Theory*. This is the idea that God inspired the concept but not the words. The writers were free to convey the concept in their own words. God gave them the idea, they chose their own words to express the idea.

*Partial Inspiration*. According to this theory, there are sections of Scripture (the revelatory portions) which are true, but most of the historical, geographical, and scientific statements are not true.

*The Neoorthodox View of Inspiration of Naturalistic Theory*. As previously mentioned, Rudolf Bultmann believed the Bible was written in mythological language. He believed the task of the modern Christian was to take out the myths in order to discover the truth.

Another branch of the Neoorthodox view is represented by men like Karl Barth and Emil Brunner. Barth said the Bible is the *locus* of God.[2] By that term he meant that God speaks to man through the Bible in a personal way. A passage may be "inspired" so far as one reader is concerned and uninspired to another. Inspiration is defined existentially. According to this idea, the Bible *becomes* the Word of God only when God is experienced through its pages.

These views demonstrate the problem of biblical revelation. How then should one view the Scriptures and what is the correct definition of inspiration?

## Plenary Verbal Inspiration

Some believe the Bible is inspired in the same way as Homer's Odyssey, Mohammed's Koran, Dante's Divine Comedy, or Shakespeare's tragedies. They believe that the writers of the Bible were smart men who had an exceptional view of life and were "inspired" by events and impressions that surrounded them.

If this idea is true, then why did these smart men write a book that condemns man? It is not likely that smart men would write a book condemning themselves along with everybody else. The Bible attacks the very things which people take pride in and the things in which human nature glorifies. This is simply not characteristic of human authors.

No, the writers of the Bible were not smart men if the Bible is uninspired, nor were they good men, because good men would not write a book full of lies giving people false hope. However, if they were bad men, how do we explain the fact that the Bible has such a high moral standard? Would bad men set the standards of morality so high? Of course not, bad men would try to justify their own badness. So if good men would not write it and bad men could not write it, from whence came the Scriptures?

The Bible makes the following claims for itself:

> For no prophecy was ever made by an act of human will, but men moved by the Holy Spirit spoke from God (2 Peter 1:21).

> Now we have received, not the spirit of the world, but the Spirit who is from God, that we might know the things freely given to us by God, which things we also speak, not in words taught by human wisdom, but in those taught by the Spirit, combining spiritual thoughts with spiritual words (1 Corinthians 2:12, 13).

> Now they have come to know that everything Thou hast given Me is from Thee; for the words which Thou gavest Me I have given to them; and they received them and truly understood that I came

forth from Thee, and they believed that Thou didst send Me (John 17:7, 8).

For I would have you know, brethren, that the gospel which was preached by me is not according to man. For I neither received it from man, nor was I taught it, but I received it through a revelation of Jesus Christ (Galatians 1:11, 12).

If anyone thinks he is a prophet or spiritual, let him recognize that the things which I write to you are the Lord's commandment (1 Corinthians 14:37).

In the Old Testament the phrases "Thus saith the Lord," "The word of the Lord came," "God said," etc., are used over 3,800 times. From Genesis to Revelation, the Bible claims its origin from God.

Still the mystery is how did God inspire the men to write the message? Did He dictate the message, thus bypassing their minds, or did He allow them freedom to choose their words? Dr. J. I. Packer sets forth the antinomy clearly:

Some moderns doubt whether this control could leave room for any free mental activity on the writers' part, and pose a dilemma: either God's control of the writers was complete, in which case they wrote as robots or automata (which clearly they did not), or their minds worked freely as they wrote the scriptures, in which case God could not fully have controlled them, or kept them from error.[3]

## God Has Spoken

At this point our faith must take over. We may never be able to reason out the "how" of biblical inspiration. The Bible clearly claims to be a full (plenary), word-for-word (verbal), God-breathed Book. Dr. Charles Ryrie defines inspiration as, "God's superintendence of the human authors so that, using their own individual personalities, they composed and recorded without error His revelation to man in the words of the original authographs."[4] Adding to this thought, Dr. Packer observes, "Instead of imposing on God arbitrary limitations of this sort, we should rather adore the wisdom and power that could so order the unruly minds of sinful men as to cause them freely and spontaneously, with no inhibiting of their normal mental processes, to write only and wholly the infallible truth of God."[5]

It is important to understand the meaning of the word "infallible," as is used by Dr. Packer. The word "inerrant" is a synonym. It means "exempt from error." The Bible is trustworthy because it contains God's truth, free from error or deception.

This definition of infallibility applies *only* to the original manuscripts of the Bible, not to the copies or translations. Surely no one would claim that the King James Version or the American Standard Version are inerrant. We cannot even claim that the critical texts, such as Westcott-Hort, the Textus Receptus, the United Bible Societies, the Nestle's, the Tasker, or the footnotes in the various texts are infallible.

Because God has promised to preserve His Word, we can believe that the translations which we have today are virtually infallible. By that I mean they are a remarkably close approximation to the original inspired manuscripts.

Edward J. Young gives a very good illustration of the difference between the original manuscripts and later copies:

> Suppose that a schoolteacher writes a letter to the President of the United States. To her great joy she receives a personal reply. It is a treasure which she must share with her pupils and so she dictates the letter to them. They are in the early days of their schooling, and spelling is not yet one of their strong points. In his copy of the letter Johnny has misspelled a few words. Mary has forgotten to cross her t's and to dot her i's. Billy has written one or two words twice, and Peter has omitted a word now and then. Nevertheless, despite all these flaws about thirty copies of the President's letter have been made. Unfortunately, the teacher misplaces the original and cannot find it. To her great sorrow it is gone. She does not have the copy which came directly

from the President's pen; she must be content with those that the children have made.

Will anyone deny that she has the words of the President? Does she not have his message, in just those words in which he wrote it to her? True enough, there are some minor mistakes in the letters, but the teacher may engage in the science of textual criticism and correct them. She may correct the misspelled words, and she may write in those words which have been omitted and cross out those which are superfluous. Without any serious difficulty she may indeed restore the original.

It should be clear that errors are bound to appear in almost anything that is copied. If the reader will copy out five pages of his English Bible he will doubtless make the discovery, on reading over his work, that he has made some mistakes. This does not mean that there are mistakes in the Bible but merely that there are some mistakes of copying (copyist's errors, as they are called) in what the reader has written out.[6]

In 1707 John Mill estimated that there were 30,000 variants (textual errors) in the New Testament alone. F. H. A. Scrivenel in 1874 counted 150,000 variants. Today critics claim there are over 200,000 errors. This sounds as if the Bible is full of errors; however, we need to realize that if a word is misspelled in 3,000 different manuscripts, then it is counted as 3,000 variants. The 200,000 variants represent only about 10,000 places in the New Testament and only about one-sixtieth rise above the level of trivialities. The fact is the New Testament text which we have today is over 99 percent pure. In view of the fact that we have over 5,000 Greek manuscripts, and some 9,000 versions and translations, the evidence for the integrity of the New Testament is overwhelming.

It is important to realize that not a single doctrinal point in the entire New Testament is affected by a disputed reading. Another point to be made clear is that the extant manuscripts are not separated by a great gap of hundreds of years from the originals. We have the four gospels (Matthew, Mark, Luke, and John) in papyrus books written before A.D. 200, little over a century after the originals. There is a fragment of the Gospel of John found in Upper Egypt, dated as early as A.D. 125. There is also a document called *The Unknown Gospel* discovered a generation ago, written before A.D. 150. It draws heavily from all four gospels, thus proving that they had already reached a place of prominence by that date. The fact that the interval between the original compositions and the earliest extant evidence is very short removes any doubt about the authenticity of our present Scriptures. We can believe that what we have today is very close to what was written originally.

## Toward a Definition

It is reasonable and scriptural to believe that God controlled and directed the men as they willingly chose the words and messages of the Bible. In that sense we can say that God inspired every word of the Bible. God, through His infinite power, was able to utilize each person's vocabulary, personality, emotions, and education in order to convey the messages which God desired. The words were the author's, but in reality, his life was God's. God developed the author's life in such a way that in reality the words he wrote were God's words. His thoughts were God's thoughts. Therefore, we can say John wrote Revelation just as surely as we can say God wrote it, and in both cases we are correct.

This fact is illustrated in the statement which Jesus made about riches. In Mark's quotation, Jesus said, "It is easier for a camel to go through the eye of a needle than for a rich man to enter the kingdom of God" (Mark 10:25). The word that Mark and Matthew used for needle is "rhaphis," which means a regular sewing needle. Luke, the physician, recorded the same statement, but instead of "rhaphis," he used the word "belone,"which means a surgeon's needle. Here is an example of God using the personality, education, and thinking process of the author to convey a message of truth. Luke was free to choose a word that conveyed the thought, but his choice of words was superintended by God.

The following quotation from A. A. Hodge and B. B. Warfield presents what I believe to be a proper understanding of inspiration.

> We believe that the great majority of those who object to the affirmation that Inspiration is verbal are impelled thereto by a feeling, more or less definite, that the phrase implies that Inspiration is, in its essence, a process of verbal dictation, or that, at least in some way, the revelation of the thought, or the inspiration of the writer, was by means of the control which God exercised over his words. And there is the more excuse for this misapprehension because of the extremely mechanical conceptions of Inspiration maintained by many former advocates of the use of this term "verbal." This view, however, we repudiate as earnestly as any of those who object to the language in question. At the present time the advocates of the strictest doctrine of Inspiration, in insisting that it is verbal, do not mean that, in any way, the thoughts were inspired by means of the words, but simply that the divine superintendence, which we call Inspiration, extended to the verbal expression of the thoughts of the sacred writers, as well to the thoughts themselves, and that, hence, the Bible considered as a record, an utterance in words of a divine revelation is the Word of God to us. Hence, in all the affirmation of Scripture of every kind, there is no more error in words of the original autographs than in the thoughts they were chosen to express. The thoughts and words are both human, and therefore, subject to human limitations, but the divine superintendence and guarantee extends to the one as much as to the other.[7]

The authority of the Bible is based on its inspiration. If we take seriously its claim of inspiration (i.e., breathed forth from

God), then we must allow it to speak to the needs of our life and respect its instructions and guidance. Only then can the Word of God find its proper place in our lives.

## Notes

[1]J. I. Packer, *God Has Spoken* (Downers Grove. IL: Inter Varsity Press, 1979), p. 98.

[2]Karl Barth, Church Dogmatics, Vol. 1, *Doctrine of The Word of God* (Naperville, IL: Allenson, 1956), pp. 592-95.

[3]Packer, p. 99

[4]Charles Caldwell Ryrie, *A Survey of Bible Doctrine* (Chicago: Moody Press, 1972), p. 38.

[5]Packer, p. 100.

[6]Edward J. Young, *Thy Word Is Truth* (Grand Rapids, MI: Wm. B. Eerdmans Publishing Co., 1957), p. 57.

[7]A. A. Hodge and B. B. Warfield, "Inspiration," *The Presbyterian Review*, No. 6, April 1881, pp. 232-233.

## Remembering the Facts

1. What is the one theme developed in the Bible from Genesis to Revelation?

2. There are several theories of biblical inspiration. Give a brief definition of the following:

   Mechanical or Dictation:

   Concept or Dynamic:

Partial Inspiration:


Neoorthodox or Naturalistic:


3. What is the correct view of inspiration as presented by Scripture?


4. What is the meaning of the word "infallible"?


5. When we speak of the Bible as being infallible, to what specifically does this apply?


6. Critics claim there are 200,000 errors in the Bible. What is one factor that makes this figure so high?


7. How many Greek manuscripts are available today?


8. How could God inspire the authors of Scripture without mechanically dictating every word?


9. Why are Mark 10:25 and Luke 18:25 good examples of how God did not dictate the Bible word for word?


10. Where does the Bible derive its authority?

## Discussing the Issues

1. Why is the subject of inspiration so important in relation to the authority of the Bible?

2. Over the years scholars have developed various theories of inspiration. Why do you think man has such difficulty in accepting the divine origin of Scripture?

3. The Bible reveals the sinfulness of many of its characters. Why do you think God is so careful to reveal both the good and bad in His people's lives?

4. Why do you think some people view the Bible as sacred in itself rather than seeing it as a revelation of God's will?

## Chapter 6
# God's Sovereignty—Total or Partial Control?

I know that Thou canst do all things, and that no purpose of Thine can be thwarted (Job 42:2).

And the Lord said, "I will blot man whom I have created from the face of the land, from man to animals to creeping things and to birds of the sky; for I am sorry that I have made them" (Genesis 6:7).

"We can never have too big a conception of God, and the more scientific knowledge (in whatever field) advances, the greater becomes our idea of His vast and complicated wisdom." So observed J. B. Phillips in his excellent little book *Your God Is Too Small*.[1]

Most people have an inadequate concept of God. Their idea of God is perhaps one which they developed as a small child. Childhood impressions are not easily discarded. As a matter of fact, many of our childhood attitudes and impressions are carried over into adulthood, and many times they create real problems in later years. Psychology has developed various therapies to help people get in touch with their childhood experiences in order to understand why they act the way they do. The value of going back into our early experiences in order to understand ourselves better cannot be denied.

This journey back into our history can be extremely valuable in relation to our belief about God. The fact is, our belief about God's nature affects our character and the way we act, live, and worship. If our information about God is faulty, it is likely that our lifestyle will also be faulty. It is of utmost importance that we hold a correct understanding of God's nature.

This chapter, perhaps more than any other, will challenge the reader's understanding about God, because we are going to explore the antinomy of God's sovereignty and man's free will. We are going to challenge the reader to reexamine his understanding concerning both of these subjects. It is a thrilling and challenging journey, so let's begin.

## God's Sovereignty

When we talk of God's sovereignty, we are saying that God is the Ruler who is in complete control of His creation. He is able to do as He pleases. "Whatever the Lord pleases, He does, in heaven and in earth, in the seas and in all deeps" (Psalm 135:6) There is no question about the fact that God is in total control of the universe.

"Have you not heard? Long ago I did it; from ancient times I planned it. Now I have brought it to pass" (2 Kings 19:25). "God is not a man, that He should lie, nor a son of man, that He should repent; has He said, and will He not do it? Or has He spoken, and will He not make it good?" (Numbers 23:19). These verses tell us that God's will is always being done. Things are working according to His plan.

Things don't just happen; they come about because God plans the events of this world to happen as they do, controlling even those things that are evil. "For truly in this city there were gathered together against Thy holy servant Jesus, whom Thou didst anoint, both Herod and Pontius Pilate, along with the Gentiles and the peoples of Israel, *to do whatever Thy hand and Thy purpose predestined to occur*" (Acts 4:27, 28; emphasis added). "The king's heart is like channels of water in the hand of the Lord; He turns it wherever He wishes" (Proverbs 21:1). " 'Can I not, O house of Israel, deal with you as this potter does?' declares the Lord. 'Behold, like the clay in the potter's hand, so are you in My hand, O house of Israel' " (Jeremiah 18:6). "He chose us in Him before the foundation of the world . . . we have obtained an inheritance, having been predestined according to His purpose who works all things after the counsel of His will" (Ephesians 1:4, 11).

When God preplans an event, the event is done though the actual carrying out of the event may still need to happen. An example of this truth is Revelation 13:8, "And all who dwell on the earth will worship him, every one whose name has not been written from the foundation of the world in the book of life of the Lamb who has been slain." The King James Version has the words "from the foundation of the world" modifying the verb "slain." It really doesn't matter if the names were written "before the foundation of the world" (see Revelation 17:8), or if Christ was slain "before the foundation of the world." The point is the same in either case. God planned man's redemption before He created the world, and His purpose was accomplished before the actual event transpired. The language indicates that God considered the event already accomplished before it happened.

It is difficult for finite minds to grasp the greatness of God, especially His sovereignty. We tend to limit God's knowledge and control because of our own limitations. We need to realize that God is bigger than any explanation of Him. Someone has said, "God created man in His own image, and man returned the favor."

Although we may not be able to understand fully His divine power and Godhead, it may help us to realize that God is outside the realm of time. We move along on a time line that consists of the past, present, and future. However, the God of the Bible created time and exists outside time. Thus all events on this earth, whether past, present, or future, are in the present with Him. God is the "Eternal Now." When God revealed Himself to Moses He said, "I Am who I Am" (Exodus 3:14). Jesus identified Himself as having the same eternal quality. Jesus said, "Truly, truly, I say to you, before Abraham was born, I Am" (John 8:58).

God can exist in many different time zones at once. "For a thousand years in Thy sight are like yesterday when it passes by, or as a watch in the night" (Psalm 90:4). Note the three different times mentioned in this verse:

1. 1,000 years—8,736,000 hours
2. Yesterday—24 hours
3. A watch in the night—3 hours

This verse tells us that time is irrelevant so far as God is concerned. All the events that have transpired on this earth, or those presently taking place, and all the events of the future are before God at this very moment. Every event, however insignificant, is before God as an eternity. A. W. Tozer observes, "In one unified present glance He comprehends all things from everlasting, and the flutter of a seraph's wing and a thousand ages hence is seen by Him now without moving His eyes."[2]

It is hard for human beings to imagine that God views time differently from us. Yet the Bible reveals the fact that God is outside space and time. We see history in a sequential series of events, but God sees all events at once—in a flash—from the beginning of time to the end.

To help us better understand this phenomenal aspect of God's relationship to time, think of the sun. It is 93 million miles away. The light from the sun, traveling at the speed of 186,000 miles per second, takes 500 seconds to reach earth. So the light that reaches earth from the sun, say, at 4:00 p.m. actually left the sun at about 3:52 p.m. If the sun suddenly vanished, you would not know it until eight minutes after it happened.

But imagine this—suppose you were in a position where you could observe both the sun and earth from outer space. You would be able to glance at the sun and earth at once and observe events at the same time. Your consciousness spans both equally. If the sun suddenly disappeared, you would know about it instantly, although the people living on earth would not know about it until eight minutes later.

Now, let's expand this concept some more. Suppose you are in a position to observe a star in the Andromeda galaxy billions of miles away and still be able to see the earth. The star you are watching all of a sudden explodes and vanishes. You would know about it immediately, although on earth that knowledge would not be known for millions of years.

When we use the word "foreknowledge" in connection with God's view of time, we must realize that it encompasses the whole universe from beginning to end. That drastically changes our understanding of God's sovereignty and man's free will. The quantum explanation of consciousness affecting matter will be explored further in the chapter dealing with prayer. The important point to emphasize is that God is capable of seeing events on this earth from a "far away view."

The day of your birth and the day of your death and every event in between are before God's eyes this moment. "Remember the former things long past, for I am God and there is no other; I am God and there is no one like me, *declaring the end from the beginning* and from ancient times things which have not been done, saying, 'My purpose will be established, and I will accomplish all my good pleasure' " (Isaiah 46:9, 10; emphasis added).

Because God's knowledge and control of the universe are perfect, there is no such thing as chance or accident. "The lot is cast into the lap, but its every decision is from the Lord" (Proverbs 16:33). This verse tells us that the most capricious of human acts is controlled by the sovereign God.

His perfect knowledge and control were emphasized by Jesus on several occasions. In Matthew 10:29-31, Jesus made the following statements. "Are not two sparrows sold for a cent? And yet not one of them will fall to the ground apart from your Father. But the very hairs of your heard are all numbered. Therefore do not fear; you are of more value than many sparrows."

During Jesus' day, sparrows were bought for hors d'oeuvres. Two were sold for the price of a penny. Luke 12:6 tells us that five sparrows sold for two pennies. Apparently they sold cheaper in large quantities. The sparrows would be roasted and served as a finger food. The point Jesus is making is that God knows when a cheap little bird falls to the ground and in fact is in control of the event.

In addition, Jesus tells us that God has numbered the hairs on our head. The average is about 140,000 hairs per head. Note that Jesus did not say that God counts them, but rather He numbers them. That means He actually identifies every hair. God's knowledge and control are much greater than what most of us have ever considered. What great comfort to know that God is in total control of every event that transpires in the universe!

## Human Responsibility

The question concerning man's free will is: How can man be free to choose if God is in total control of all events? Isn't man just a puppet on a string with every action directed and controlled by God? This is perhaps one of the most difficult of all the biblical antinomies to understand. Many controversies have arisen down through the centuries over this issue. Augustine debated with the Pelagians, who overemphasized human responsibility almost to the exclusion of God's sovereignty.

More recently the controversy has continued between Calvinism and Arminianism. Calvinists believe in divine sovereignty because human beings are incapable of choosing to believe or obey God. Therefore, God, not the individual, must initiate the relationship. The five points of Calvinism are:

*Total Depravity.* The sinner is dead, blind, and deaf to the things of God. His heart is deceitful and corrupt. He is not free but rather in bondage to his evil nature. Faith is not a matter of choice; it is God's gift to the sinner.

*Unconditional Election.* God's choice is based on His sovereign will. It is not based on any forseen response of obedience on the sinner's part. On the contrary, God gives to each individual the faith, repentance, etc. necessary to accept Christ. God's choice and not the sinner's is the ultimate cause of salvation.

*Limited Atonement.* The substitutionary death of Christ on the cross was intended to save the elect only. Christ's redemption purchased everything necessary for salvation including the sinner's obedience.

*Irresistible Graced.* Those who are sovereignly elected to salvation will never fail to respond to God's call. The Holy Spirit irresistibly draws the sinner to Christ. The sinner does not cooperate in any way.

*Perseverance of Saints.* Not only does the sinner respond irresistibly to God's grace, but he also remains in a saved condition. The sinner, thus redeemed, is kept in faith by God's power and will persevere to the end. These five points were adopted during the Synod of Dort (Dortrecht) in 1619. They became the official doctrine of the State Church of the Netherlands and later the Reformed Church of France, the Puritans, and the Reformed Dutch Church in America.

According to the Calvinistic concept of sovereignty, God touches the heart of the sinner. The Holy Spirit makes the death of Christ effective by bringing the elect to faith and repentance, thereby causing them to willingly obey. The entire process of salvation is based on God's sovereign control of all events.

Here we find one of the great mysteries of the Bible . . . the mystery of human responsibility. The Bible teaches that while God controls all events in His creation; nevertheless, He has given man freedom to choose his own action. "The Lord is not slow about His promise, as some count slowness, but is patient toward you, not wishing for any to perish but for all to come to repentance" (2 Peter 3:9). "This is good and acceptable in the sight of God our Savior, who desires all men to be saved and to come to the knowledge of the truth" (1 Timothy 2:3, 4). " 'Do I have any pleasure in the death of the wicked,' declares the Lord God, 'rather than that he should turn from his ways and live?' " (Ezekiel 18:23).

These verses indicate that God desires the salvation of all people. If God wishes that all people would come to repentance, then obviously, in His sovereign will, it would seem that He would bring all men to repentance. If God takes pleasure in the wicked turning from His ways, then why does He allow the wicked to continue in sin? "Whatever the Lord pleases, He does, in heaven and in earth. . . ." (Psalm 135:6).

Jesus said, "Come to Me, all who are weary and heavy-laden, and I will give you rest" (Matthew 11:28). The invitation suggests that the heavy-laden have a choice; they may refuse to receive rest.

Some passages of Scripture intertwine both concepts in a marvelous way. The following example in John 6 is a good illustration.

## God's Sovereignty

All that the Father gives Me shall come to Me; and the one who comes to Me I will certainly not cast out (verse 37).

No one can come to Me, unless the Father who sent Me draws him; and I will raise him up on the last day (verse 44).

And He was saying, "For this reason I have said to you, that no one can come to Me, unless it has been granted him from the Father" (verse 65).

## Man's Responsibility

Jesus answered and said to them, "This is the work of God, that you believe in Him whom He has sent" (verse 29).

Jesus said to them, "I am the bread of life; he who comes to Me shall not hunger, and he who believes in Me shall never thirst" (verse 35).

For this is the will of My Father, that everyone who beholds the Son, and believes in Him, may have eternal life; and I Myself will raise him up on the last day (verse 40).

Truly, truly, I say to you, he who believes has eternal life (verse 47).

Another example is Jeremiah 18:1-12:

The word which came to Jeremiah from the Lord saying, "Arise and go down to the potter's house, and there I shall announce My words to you." Then I went down to the potter's house, and there he was, making something on the wheel. But the vessel that he was making of clay was spoiled in the hand of the potter; so he remade it into another vessel, as it pleased the potter to make. Then the word of the Lord came to me saying, "Can I not, O house of Israel, deal with you as this potter does?" declares the Lord. "Behold, like the clay in the potter's hand, so are you in My hand, O house of Israel. At one moment I might speak concerning a nation or concerning a kingdom to uproot, to pull down, or to destroy it; if that nation against which I have spoken turns from its evil, I will relent concerning the calamity I planned to bring on it. Or at another

moment I might speak concerning a nation or concerning a kingdom to build up or to plant it; if it does
evil in My sight by not obeying My voice, then I will
think better of the good with which I had promised
to bless it. So now then, speak to the men of Judah
and against the inhabitants of Jerusalem saying,
'Thus says the Lord, "Behold, I am fashioning calamity against you and devising a plan against you. Oh
turn back, each of you from his evil way, and reform
your ways and your deeds." ' But they will say, 'It's
hopeless! For we are going to follow our own plans,
and each of us will act according to the stubbornness
of his evil heart.' "

Still another marvelous text in which God's sovereignty and
man's free will are intertwined is Philippians 2:12, 13. "So then,
my beloved, just as you have always obeyed, not as in my presence only, but now much more in my absence, work out your own
salvation with fear and trembling; for it is God who is at work in
you, both to will and to work for His good pleasure."

Kenneth Boa observes,

In some inexplicable way God has seen fit to incorpo-
rate human freedom and responsibility into His all-
inclusive plan. Even though the Lord is in sovereign
control of the details in His creation, He never forces
any man to do anything against his will. The fact
that He judges sin means that He is not responsible
for the commission of the sins He judges. When a
person sins it is because he has freely chosen to do
so. Similarly, when someone is confronted with the
terms of the Gospel, he can freely choose to accept or
reject Christ's offer of forgiveness of sins. Because it
is a free choice, he will be held responsible for the
decision he makes (see John 12:48).[3]

## A Just Judge

"Shall not the Judge of all the earth deal justly?" (Genesis 18:25). The answer to this rhetorical question is "Yes." But the problem of how He will do it is puzzling. The question of God's sovereignty and His right to judge man was raised by the apostle Paul. "So then He has mercy on whom He desires, and He hardens whom He desires. You will say to me then, 'Why does He still find fault? For who resists His will?' " (Romans 9:18, 19). Here is the antinomy—God is sovereign—He is in complete control of man's actions, yet man is responsible to God for his deeds. How then can God blame man for his disobedience?

Peter wrote about those who disbelieve and why they are disobedient. "For they stumble because they are disobedient to the word, and to this doom they were also appointed" (1 Peter 2:8). The Bible also declares, "The Lord has made everything for its own purpose, even the wicked for the day of evil" (Proverbs 16:4).

In our finite understanding, we might say that God is unfair in condemning those who are evil. Weren't they only pawns in a cosmic chess game of eternity? For example, what about Judas? Didn't he do what God appointed him to do when he betrayed Christ? Scripture says, "For indeed, the Son of Man is going as it has been determined; but woe to that man through whom He is betrayed!" (Luke 22:22). Peter said, "This Man, delivered up by the predetermined plan and foreknowledge of God, you nailed to a cross by the hands of godless men and put Him to death" (Acts 2:23). These verses tell us that God's "predetermined plan" was carried out and yet all who participated in His plan are held responsible for their deeds.

Paul's response to this antinomy is that we really don't have a right to question God's wisdom and sovereignty.

> Who are you, O man, who answers back to God? The thing molded will not say to the molder, "Why did you make me like this," will it? Or does not the potter have a right over the clay, to make from the same lump one vessel for honorable use, and another for common use? What if God, although willing to

> demonstrate His wrath and to make His power
> known, endured with much patience vessels of wrath
> prepared for destruction? And He did so in order
> that He might make known the riches of His glory
> upon vessels of mercy, which He prepared before-
> hand for glory (Romans 9:20-23).

Judgment will be fair and just because God's perfect knowledge and man's free choice will be considered in connection with
God's eternal plan. No one will argue with God about the outcome.

Jesus gave further insight into God's judgment in Matthew
11:20-24.

> Then He began to reproach the cities in which most
> of His miracles were done, because they did not
> repent: "Woe to you, Chorazin! Woe to you,
> Bethsaida! For if the miracles had occurred in Tyre
> and Sidon which occurred in you, they would have
> repented long ago in sackcloth and ashes. Neverthe-
> less I say to you, it shall be more tolerable for Tyre
> and Sidon in the day of judgment, than for you. And
> you, Capernaum, will not be exalted to heaven, will
> you? You shall descend to Hades; for if the miracles
> had occurred in Sodom which occurred in you, it
> would have remained to this day. Nevertheless I say
> to you that it shall be more tolerable for the land of
> Sodom in the day of judgment, than for you."

This tremendous text reveals several things about God's
judgment.

1. Men will be held accountable for their actions.
2. The Lord already knows what will happen on the judgment
   day because of His infinite knowledge.
3. He not only knows what did happen, but what would have
   happened under different circumstances.

4. The knowledge of what might have been under different circumstances will be taken into consideration on judgment day.

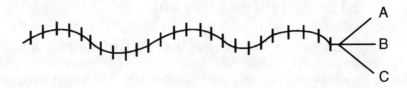

*Figure No. 4*

Figure 4 represents the time line of a person's life at a particular point at which he must choose between three decisions. God knows before the choice is made what decision the individual will make. God also knows what the outcome of that decision will be as well as what the outcome of the other two decisions would be. The amazing part of all this is God can take the person's decision and make that decision a part of His eternal plan for that person's life. If the decision is not to believe in God, the individual will be held responsible for his choice on the day of judgment. Whatever choice he makes, God will use that choice to complete His perfect plan for the individual's life. On the day of judgment, God will take into consideration not only the choice that was made under the circumstances prevalent, but also the decision that would have been made if the circumstances were different. God's infinite knowledge and divine sovereignty will guarantee a righteous and just judgment.

Although difficult to explain or understand, the antinomy of God's sovereignty brings some real blessings into our lives: (1) A deeper worship. How can we worship a God that is thwarted by the sins of man and the power of Satan? On the other hand, if we can see a God that truly rules in the affairs of men and constantly controls and directs His universe, we can joyfully bow down in reverence before Him and live lives of obedient service to Him. (2) A great comfort in trials. Christians, as well as non-Christians, experience trials and temptations. If we try to face these difficulties on our own, we are doomed to defeat. However, if we meet these trials and temptations with faith in a sovereign Lord who we believe is in control of our lives and the circumstances around us, then we can find the strength to endure, even while we may not understand why we must suffer. (3) A greater evangelistic spirit. We can be bold in evangelism if we believe that God's sovereign power is working with us to take the message to the elect. On the other hand, if we feel that we must go in our own power, surely our strength will fail us! (4) A grater security. Even though we may never understand the antinomy of God's sovereignty, we can rest assured that He is with us always, even to the end of the age (Matthew 28:20). What greater security could there be than to know that the great God who created this world is on my side and will never forsake me (Rom. 8:31, 35, 37-39)!

There are some wonderful promises in Scripture which are fulfilled by God's sovereign control: Hebrews 7:25 "Hence, also, He is able to save forever those who draw near to God through Him, since He always lives to make intercession for them." 2 Timothy 1:12 "For this reason I also suffer these things, but I am not ashamed; for I know whom I have believed and I am convinced that He is able to guard what I have entrusted to Him until that day." 2 Corinthians 9:8 "And God is able to make all grace abound to you, that always having all sufficiency in everything, you may have an abundance for every good deed." Hebrews 2:18 "For since He Himself was tempted in that which He has suffered, He is able to come to the aid of those who are tempted." 1 Corinthians 10:13 "No temptation has overtaken you but such as is common to man; and God is faithful, who will not allow you to be tempted beyond what you are able, but with the temptation will provide the way of escape also, that you may be able to endure it." Ephesians 3:20, 21 "Now to Him who is able to do exceeding abundantly beyond all that we ask or think, according to the power that works within us, to Him be the glory in the church and in Christ Jesus to all generations forever and forever. Amen!" Philippians 3:21 "Who will transform the body of our humble state into conformity with the body of His glory by the exertion of the power that He has even to subject all things to Himself." Jude 24-25 "Now to Him who is able to keep you from stumbling, and to make you stand in the presence of His glory blameless with great joy, to the only God our Savior, through Jesus Christ our Lord, be glory, majesty, dominion and authority, before all time and now and forever. Amen."

When we begin to explore the depths of God's wisdom, power, and understanding, we must say with the Psalmist, "Such knowledge is too wonderful for me; it is too high, I cannot obtain it" (Psalm 139:6).

We have only touched the "hem of the garment" concerning the God's sovereignty/human responsibility antinomy. Our finite understanding prevents a full comprehension of the problem. By faith we must accept the biblical revelation of both truths. Maintaining a proper balance between the extremes will prevent our denying a truth which God's Word affirms.

## Notes

[1]J. B. Phillips, *Your God Is Too Small* (New York: The Macmillan Company, 1961), pp. 120-121.

[2]A. W. Tozer, *The Divine Conquest* (Harrisburg: Christian Publications, 1950), p. 21.

[3]Kenneth Boa, *God, I Don't Understand* (Wheaton, IL: Victor Books, 1979), pp. 51-52. Many of the concepts in this book were gained from a study of the excellent work contained in Boa's book. I highly recommend it for those interested in studying biblical antinomies.

## Remembering the Facts

1. What is the meaning of sovereignty?

2. Why do we tend to limit in our minds God's knowledge and control?

3. What is God's relationship to time?

4. Matthew 10:24-31 is a good illustration of God's total control of His creation. Write a brief commentary on this text in your own words.

5. Calvinists believe in divine sovereignty to the exclusion of free choice. Write the five points of doctrine that compose Calvinistic theology:

    (1)

    (2)

    (3)

    (4)

    (5)

6. Why is Matthew 11:28 a good example of free choice?

7. Matthew 11:20-24 teaches that God's judgment will be fair and just. Explain why this is true.

8. How is it possible for God to take every decision we make and use it to fulfill His plan?

9. When the Psalmist began to contemplate the magnitude of God's greatness, what did he say (Psalm 139:6)?

10. How can we maintain a proper balance with regard to God's sovereignty and man's free will?

## Discussing the Issues

1. Why is it important to hold a correct view of God's nature?

2. In view of God's sovereignty, how should the Christian view the people in a "far away land" who have never heard the gospel?

3. If our view of people in a "far away land" is one that accepts their condition as hopeless, why should we personally be concerned for their welfare or salvation?

4. How should the sovereignty of God and man's free will affect the way we persuade people to believe in Christ?

# Chapter 7
# Forgiveness—By Works or Grace?

> For by grace you have been saved through faith; and that not of yourselves, it is the gift of God; not as a result of works, that no one should boast (Ephesians 2:8, 9).
>
> You see that a man is justified by works, and not by faith alone (James 2:24).

Every good book should have at least one main objective or purpose for its existence. If I were to choose one goal for this book, it would be to assist the reader in finding a proper balance with regard to the biblical antinomies.

The desire to reach that goal finds its most difficult challenge in the area we are about to face in this chapter—the balance between grace and works. It is in this area that Martin Luther found his greatest struggle. Many debates among theologians have been conducted down through the centuries in an effort to resolve this antinomy.

Perhaps the reason this antinomy has been so controversial is that it deals with the most important aspect of our relationship with God—the forgiveness of sins. It affects our eternal salvation and it deals with our everyday experience. The knowledge of how forgiveness is obtained is of utmost importance in order to live a secure, joyful Christian life. Without this knowledge, we are left with no certain assurance that we are forgiven by God, thus our eternal destiny is left in limbo.

Most of the controversies of the New Testament church centered around this issue. In Acts 15, the Jerusalem council had to deal with this issue because "some men came down from Judea and began teaching the brethren, 'Unless you are circum-

cised according to the custom of Moses, you cannot be saved' "
(Acts 15:1).

Almost anyone who studies carefully the teachings of the
New Testament will have to admit that salvation is based on
God's grace. But understanding how works fit into the picture is
a difficult task.

## Understanding Grace

Grace has been defined in several ways. The primary definition of grace is "God's unmerited favor." Grace is the eternal and
absolutely free favor of God, manifested in the giving of spiritual
and eternal blessing to the guilty through the atoning sacrifice
of Christ. God's act of grace is the provision of something needed
but not deserved.

But why does man need undeserved favor? The answer lies
in the condition of man's heart toward God. God created man
with the freedom to choose the course or direction of his life (see
chapter 4). Adam and Eve were placed in a perfect environment
that was especially suited for their happiness and well-being.
God gave the following restriction, "From any tree of the garden
you may eat freely; but from the tree of the knowledge of good
and evil you shall not eat, for in the day that you eat from it you
shall surely die" (Genesis 2:16, 17). Some may ask, "Why the
restriction?" The answer lies in the relationship that existed
between God and man. It was a relationship of love, similar to
that between parent and child. Every relationship of love between parent and child must involve obedience on the part of the
child. Without obedience, love cannot be expressed.

The restriction God placed on the "tree of the knowledge of
good and evil" was an act of love on God's part. It provided an
avenue for Adam and Eve to express their trust, confidence,
obedience, and love toward God. How else could physical beings
relate to a Spiritual Being?

Adam and Eve no doubt had some knowledge of evil before
they violated God's prohibition. However, the moment they dis-
obeyed God's command, they experienced that knowledge in

their lives (guilt, shame, disgrace, et. al.). Francis Schaeffer observes, "In the case of Adam and Eve, as finite, they had received from God true knowledge concerning the result of eating and revolt, but when they did revolt they then had experiential knowledge of evil and all the flow of resulting cruelty and sorrow. It was not knowledge as knowledge that was wrong, but the choice made, against God's loving warning and command."[1]

The result of that choice was alienation from God because a holy, righteous God cannot tolerate nor fellowship that which is antagonistic to His nature. Disobedience is the opposite of love. Man chose to go away from God. The result is a condition of lostness. That condition is described in various ways in the Bible:

> Being darkened in their understanding, excluded from the life of God, because of the ignorance that is in them, because of the hardness of their hearts; and they, having become callous, have given themselves over to sensuality, for the practice of every kind of impurity with greediness (Ephesians 4:18, 19).

> What is the source of quarrels and conflicts among you? Is not the source your pleasures that wage war in your members? (James 4:1).

> For they exchanged the truth of God for a lie, and worshiped and served the creature rather than the Creator, who is blessed forever (Romans 1:25).

> You ask and do not receive, because you ask with wrong motives, so that you may spend it on your pleasures (James 4:3).

> For not knowing about God's righteousness, and seeking to establish their own, they did not subject themselves to the righteousness of God (Romans 10:3).

> The fool has said in his heart, "There is no God." They are corrupt, they have committed abominable deeds; there is no one who does good (Psalm 14:1).

The condition of man since the fall is of such nature that God, in His righteousness, justice, and purity, is unable to forgive until in His own judicial counsel sin has been properly punished. The plan for man's redemption was established and settled in eternity when God planned for man's creation. God knew beforehand that man would need a redeemer. The answer to man's sin problem has always been the atoning sacrifice of Jesus Christ in order to establish God's justice and satisfy His judicial requirements.

I've often wondered if there ever was a time that God did not know that He would create man. I doubt there was. For as long as God has existed, which is forever, He probably knew that He would create man, that man would willingly choose to disobey, that Christ would die on the cross for our sins, and that you and I would either accept the message of truth or reject it. Such knowledge is beyond our ability to comprehend; however, it is important to realize that God did not have a variety of plans to choose from in order to provide forgiveness for mankind. There was only one way man could be forgiven judicially and that was through the death of Christ.

God began preparation for man's redemption immediately after Adam and Eve rebelled. To Satan God said, "I will put enmity between you and the woman, and between your seed and her seed; he shall bruise you on the head, and you shall bruise him on the heel" (Genesis 3:15). This verse has been called the *protevangelium* because it is the first announcement concerning Christ's defeat of Satan. The prophecy was that Christ, the seed of woman, would totally destroy Satan with a crushing blow to the head while Satan would only inflict a minor wound to His heel. Both aspects of this prophecy were fulfilled by Christ on the cross. The bruise to the heel took place in the cruel torture inflicted on God's Son by the ordeal of the cross; the bruise to Satan's head came when Christ was triumphantly raised from the dead. The all-encompassing power of Christ's resurrection is set forth clearly by Paul in Ephesians 1:19b-21, "These are in accordance with the working of the strength of His might which He brought about in Christ, when He raised Him from the dead, and seated Him at His right hand in the heavenly places, far above all rule and authority and power and dominion, and every name that is named, not only in this age, but also in the one to come." There is no power or authority equal to that which Christ possesses.

The work which Christ performed in His total obedience to God's law and sacrificial death on the cross accomplished (earned or merited) salvation for all mankind. The doing and dying of Jesus were performed both for God and man. "This was to demonstrate His righteousness, because in the forbearance of God He passed over the sins previously committed; for the demonstration, I say, of His righteousness at the present time, that He might be just and the justifier of the one who has faith in Jesus" (Romans 3:25, 26).

You will note carefully in this text that the propitiatory death of Christ accomplished two important things:

1. God's justice was maintained. (God's righteousness was demonstrated through the life and death of Jesus.)
2. The one who has faith in Jesus is justified (declared to be just or righteous).

Jesus Christ satisfied the demands of God's law; His death provided sufficient punishment for sin in order that, in the judicial council of God, forgiveness could be given to all who would seek God's favor. God maintained His justice while at the same time forgiving the sins of those who had violated His law. That's grace!

## God's Satisfaction

The New Testament concept of salvation is that of a ransom paid to satisfy God's requirements concerning His law and the penalty of sin. "For you have been bought with a price: therefore glorify God in your body" (1 Corinthians 6:20). "You were bought with a price; do not become slaves of men" (1 Corinthians 7:23). "Knowing that you were not redeemed with perishable things like silver or gold . . . but with precious blood . . . the blood of Christ" (1 Peter 1:18, 19). Christ's ownership of the church is the result of a purchase—the satisfaction of a ransom (Acts 20:28; Revelation 5:9).

During the eleventh century A.D., Anselm, the archbishop of Canterbury (1033-1109), developed a theology of atonement centered around the word "satisfaction." His concept, set forth in his *Cur Cens Homo*, "Why God Became Man," was that Christ satisfied divine justice by His doing and dying. This became known as the Latin or forensic theory of atonement. The Reformation Movement continued to develop this concept of the death of Christ as a "vicarious satisfaction of divine justice." Much of Western Protestantism has been dominated by Anselm's theory of atonement.

In response to Anselm, Peter Abelard (1079-1142) developed an opposing theory that has become known as the "moral-influence" theory. Abelard's concept was that God demonstrated His love, mercy, and grace at the cross in such a way that it would motivate people to repentance, faith, and obedience. According to this theory, there was no "objective transaction" at Calvary by which salvation was procured. Salvation becomes a matter of subjective experience. Many variations of this concept exist today in Western churches.

While it is true that the term "satisfaction" is not used in the sense of Christ meeting certain divine requirements on man's behalf; nevertheless, the idea is certainly present in many passages. Here is one convincing example:

> Christ redeemed us from the curse of the Law, having become a curse for us—for it is written, "Cursed is every one who hangs on a tree" (Galatians 3:13).

Note the expressions in this verse that suggest Christ "satisfied" a divine standard:

*"Christ redeemed us."* The word redeemed (Greek: exagorazo) according to Vine means, "to buy out (ex or ek), especially of purchasing a slave with a view to his freedom."[2] Christ paid the price by suffering the "curse of the law" on our behalf.

*"The curse of the Law."* God's broken law required a "curse," eventuating in death (Galations 3:13). Christ experienced the "curse" of a broken law.

*"Having become a curse for us."* Although Christ had not violated God's law, yet in a judicial sense (a legal transaction in God's court) Christ received the imputation of God's broken law. God imputed our sin to Christ and He experienced its penalty (2 Corinthians 5:21).

*"For us,"* which means "for our sakes," or "on our behalf." Charles Erdman observes, "This is the strongest possible statement of vicarious suffering."[3]

*"Cursed is everyone who hangs on a tree."* It was the custom of the Hebrews to hang the body of a criminal on a tree or post. It served as a testimony that sufficient penalty had been paid for a broken law. It was a public proclamation that sin had been punished. Christ's crucifixion served as a visual display that Christ had "satisfied" a divine penalty for sin.

Two other passages which may also be studied in connection with Christ satisfying God's requirements on our behalf are: 2 Corinthians 5:14f; 1 Peter 2:24. The prophet Isaiah wrote of God's reaction to Messiah's suffering: "As a result of the anguish of His soul, He will see it and be satisfied" (Isaiah 53:11).

John R. W. Stott sums up well the work of Christ on our behalf:

> He died for our sins, bearing them in His own innocent and sacred person. He took upon Himself our sins and their just reward. The death that Jesus died was the wages of sin—our sin. He met its claim, He paid its penalty. He accepted its reward, and He did it "once," once for all. As a result sin has no more claim or demand on Him so He was raised from the dead to prove the satisfactoriness of His sin-bearing, and He now lives forever to God.[4]

Jesus became our "substitute" because He was qualified to pay the penalty of sin based on His perfect life (unblemished and spotless—1 Peter 1:19). His life—His death—His divinity all qualified Him to be a proper "sacrifice" on our behalf. God's judicial requirements were met and divine forgiveness was procured for every person.

## On Our Behalf

What makes God's grace so amazing is the fact that what Christ accomplished, He accomplished for us. "He made Him who knew no sin to be sin *on our behalf*, that we might become the righteousness of God in Him" (2 Corinthians 5:21; emphasis added).

Note these 3 points:

1.  Christ was righteous ("He . . . knew no sin").
2.  Sin was imputed to Him ("He made Him . . . to be sin").
3.  We receive His righteousness ("that we might become the righteousness of God in Him").

Christ became what we are in order that we might become what He is. God places us in a judicial relationship with Him by clothing us with Christ (Galatians 3:26, 27). We, therefore, stand before God clothed in the righteousness of Christ.

> When He shall come with trumpet sound,
> O may I then in Him be found
> Dressed in His righteousness alone,
> Faultless to stand before the throne.

## Salvation Is a Matter of Righteousness

Salvation from sin is a matter of becoming righteous in God's sight. Alan Richardson says, "Righteousness is for the Hebrews the fundamental character of God."[5] To be righteous, therefore, means to conform to God's perfect standard. Anything less would be unrighteous. We would conclude from a study of the term "righteousness" as it is used in both testaments that the true meaning is perfect conformity to divine law.

This is why we find the terms "righteousness" and "salvation" used in very close relationship in both the Old and New Testaments.

> My righteousness is near, My salvation has gone forth (Isaiah 51:5).

> And He put on righteousness like a breastplate, and a helmet of salvation on His head (Isaiah 59:17).
>
> Thus says the Lord, "Preserve justice, and do righteousness, for My salvation is about to come" (Isaiah 56:1).
>
> For I am not ashamed of the gospel, for it is the power of God for salvation to every one who believes, to the Jew first and also to the Greek. For in it the righteousness of God is revealed from faith to faith (Romans 1:16, 17).
>
> . . . that, as sin reigned in death, even so grace might reign through righteousness to eternal life through Jesus Christ our Lord (Romans 5:21).
>
> For with the heart man believes, resulting in righteousness, and with the mouth he confesses, resulting in salvation (Romans 10:10).

Any teaching about salvation that does not relate to righteousness is missing the point.

Isaiah declared that righteousness is only in the Lord (Isaiah 45:24) and all of man's righteous deeds are like a filthy garment (Isaiah 64:6). Man's condition before God is one of rebellion and disobedience. Even his righteous deeds are corrupted by selfish motives. Man stands in a condition of unrighteousness before the righteous God of this universe.

So the question is: How can man be righteous before God? It is obvious that if man is to be righteous, his righteousness will have to come from somewhere outside himself. Even God's righteous law cannot make man righteous, "for if righteousness comes through the law, then Christ died needlessly" (Galatians 2:21).

Since man is incapable of achieving or maintaining God's righteousness, the only possible way for man to be righteous is to receive it as a gift from God. "For if by the transgression of one, death reigned through the one, much more those who receive the abundance of grace and of the *gift of righteousness* will reign in life through the One, Jesus Christ" (Romans 5:17;

emphasis added). Righteousness is a gift that is put to the credit of all who trust in Christ Jesus (Romans 4:6).

Therefore, when a person trusts in Christ, he stands in God's presence declared just and clothed with the very character of God himself. His sins and lawless deeds have been forgiven and God is able to accept him into His holy fellowship. The Christian actually becomes a participant in God's divine nature (2 Peter 1:4).

## The Importance of Works

To say that man cannot be saved from sin by his own good deeds is not the same as saying that man is saved apart from works. Even faith itself is classified a work (John 6:29). Whatever effort man exerts toward God is in its strictest sense a work, whether it is faith, repentance, baptism, or faithful Christian living. The act of faith in Christ is in fact obedience to a command. "And this is His commandment, that we believe in the name of His Son Jesus Christ. . . ." (1 John 3:23). It is impossible for man to do anything in relation to God without obedience or works.

The antinomy of grace and works becomes less of a problem when we realize that salvation from sin is always on the basis of God's grace, which is appropriated into a person's life by faith. Faith, however, is not idle. Saving faith is always accompanied by good works. As the reformers would say, "Man is saved by faith alone, but the faith that saves is never alone."

However, there are times when the New Testament seems to put faith and works in opposition to each other. Paul wrote, "For by grace you have been saved through faith . . . not as a result of works" ( Ephesians 2:8, 9). James wrote, "You see that a man is justified by works and not by faith alone" (James 2:24).

This problem is solved very easily by looking at the context of each passage. In Romans Paul dealt with the righteousness of God in contradistinction to man's righteousness. He illustrated man's decline and fall in chapters 1-3, concluding that "all have sinned and fall short of the glory of God" (Romans 3:23). In a fallen condition, apart from the righteousness of Christ, man is in a helpless, hopeless condition. There are no works man can perform that will rescue him from his fallen condition.

James, on the other hand, writes about man's relationship with God through "faith in our glorious Lord Jesus Christ" (James 2:1). James shows that genuine faith will be evident in the good works that the Christian performs because of his faith. "Even so faith, if it has no works, is dead, being by itself" (James 2:17). Good works become evidence of the genuineness of the Christian's faith.

While it is true that man cannot be saved by his good works apart from Christ; nevertheless, faith and works are inseparable insofar as man's relationship with God in Christ is concerned. What God commands the true believer will gladly obey. "Jesus answered and said to him, 'If anyone loves Me, he will keep My word' " (John 14:23). "If you love Me, you will keep My commandments" (John 14:15). Works are an outgrowth of faith; by-products of the Spirit's work in the life of a believer (Romans 8).

## Legalism or License

Maintaining a balance in the grace/works antinomy will help us avoid two serious pitfalls. One is the pitfall of legalism. The term "legalist" is often used to brand a person who believes in law-keeping. However, every Christian who loves the Lord believes in law-keeping. The legalist goes beyond law-keeping as a response to God's grace and teaches that law-keeping is that which makes one righteous in God's sight. The legalist sees the law as a means of righteousness rather than Christ.

The legalistic concept of salvation sees the law as a means to salvation through Christ whereas the biblical perspective presents law-keeping as a response to the cross. Law-keeping is an expression of love and devotion to Christ for salvation, not a means of achieving salvation in Christ. Law describes how God intends the Christian to live, and through God's Spirit the requirements of the law are fulfilled in the Christian's life (Romans 8:4).

George Thomas has presented four real dangers of legalism.[6] First, it is in large part negative and restrictive. The legalist's religion is always a matter of "don'ts." One's spirituality is gauged by the legalist in terms of what he does not do.

Second, legalism stifles individuality and creativity in conduct. Since legalism is committed to a pre-set pattern of living, there is little creative effort exerted in finding new and better ways of living.

Third, it tends to fall into externalism. Great emphasis is put on the things that one can do and be seen in the doing. It puts a premium on certain "acts" as indicators of spiritual maturity.

Fourth, it is externally imposed on the will, and when it is contrary to natural inclination, it is unable to secure obedience.

The sad consequence of legalism is that it prevents any real personal relationship to develop between believers. Brunner observes, "The legalistic type of person . . . finds it impossible to come into real human, personal contact with his fellowman. Between him and his neighbor there stands something impersonal, the 'idea,' the 'Law,' a program . . . something abstract which hinders him from seeing the other person as he really is, which prevents him from hearing the real claim which his neighbor makes on him."[7]

The other extreme is license (sometimes called *antinomianism* which means "against law"). Jude referred to those who turned "the grace of our God into licentiousness" (Jude 4). J. I. Packer observes, "Whereas the legalist so magnifies the law as to crowd out grace, the antinomian is so mesmerized by grace as to lose sight of the law as a rule of life."[8] The mature Christian will endeavor to maintain a proper balance between grace and works, avoiding the pitfalls of legalism and antinomianism, but always relying upon the Holy Spirit for strength to live an obedient life.

The magnificient truths which we have studied in this lesson are best summed up in the beautiful hymn by Augustus M. Toplady:

> Nothing in my hands I bring,
> Simply to Thy cross I cling;
> Naked, came to Thee for dress;

Helpless, look to Thee for grace;
Foul, I to the fountain fly;
Wash me, Savior, or I die.
Rock of Ages, cleft for me,
Let me hide myself in Thee.

## Notes

[1]Francis A. Schaeffer, *Genesis In Space and Time* (Downers Grove, IL: Inter Varsity Press, 1972), p. 73.

[2]W. E. Vine, *Expository Dictionary of New Testament Words* (Old Tappan, NJ: Fleming H. Revell, Co., 1940), p. 263.

[3]Charles R. Erdman, *The Epistle of Paul to the Galatians* (Philadelphia, PA: The Westminster Press, 1930), p. 72.

[4]John R. W. Stott, *Men Made New* (Downers Grove, IL: Inter Varsity Press, 1960), p. 43.

[5]Alan Richardson, *An Introduction to the Theology of the New Testament* (New York: Harper and Row, 1958), p. 79.

[6]George F. Thomas, *Christian Ethics and Moral Philosophy* (New York: Scribners Sons, 1955), p. 129.

[7]Emil Brunner, *The Divine Imperative: A Study in Christian Ethics* (Philadelphia, PA: The Westminster Press, 1947), p. 73.

[8]J. I. Packer, *God's Words* (Downers Grove, IL: Inter Varsity Press, 1981), p. 104.

## Remembering the Facts

1. Why is the subject of grace and works so controversial?

2. Write a brief definition of the meaning of grace.

3. Why did God put a restriction on the tree of the knowledge of good and evil?

4. Why is God unable to forgive sin apart from Christ?

5. Romans 3:25, 26 sets forth two important things accomplished through Christ's life and death. List them:

   (1)


   (2)


6. Write brief definitions of the Latin or forensic theory of atonement and the moral influence theory. Which is more biblical?

7. Galatians 3:13 is a convincing text which demonstrates that Christ satisfied divine requirements on man's behalf. Explain why.

8. Write some Scripture references which demonstrate that salvation is a matter of righteousness.

9. The Bible teaches man cannot be saved by his own works. How is this different from saying man is saved apart from works?

10. How does the legalistic concept of salvation view the law? Explain why this is incorrect.

## Discussing the Issues

1. Why do some people find it hard to accept salvation by grace?

2. Do you believe that a strong emphasis on God's grace will diminish or increase appreciation for works? Why?

3. "As a Christian I should believe as though everything depended on Christ and I should work as though everything depended on me." Is that statement a correct view? Why or why not?

4. For most people it is easier to go to extremes in the grace/works antinomy rather than maintain the balance. Why is this true?

# Chapter 8
# Prayer—God's Purpose or Man's Will?

If you ask Me anything in My name, I will do it (John 14:14).

Concerning this I entreated the Lord three times that it might depart from me (2 Corinthians 12:8).

Just how effective are the prayers of believers? It is reported that H. G. Wells, a critic of Christianity, once described God as "an ever-absent help in time of trouble."

The story is told of a man who bought a mountain cottage overlooking a beautiful lake. After he moved into his cottage, he discovered that there was a high hill between the lake and his front porch which blocked some of the view of the lake. So when he retired that evening, he prayed that God would remove the hill, remembering the words of Jesus, "If you have faith as a mustard seed, you shall say to this mountain, 'Move from here to there,' and it shall move." Early the next morning the man arose, rushed to the porch and discovered that the hill was there, just where it had always been. The man said, "Well, that's about what I had expected."

This story illustrates how most people view prayer—that it is an exercise in futility. Mark Twain illustrated this view in *The Adventures of Huckleberry Finn*. Huck Finn said,

> Then Miss Watson she took me in the closet and prayed, but nothing came of it. She told me to pray every day and whatever I asked for I would get it. But it warn't so. I tried it. Once I got a fish-line but no hooks. It warn't any good to me without hooks. I

tried for the hooks three or four times but somehow
I couldn't make it work. By and by, one day I asked
Miss Watson to try for me, but she said I was a fool.
She never told me why, and I couldn't make it out no
way.

I set down one time back in the woods, and had a
long think about it. I says to myself, if a body can get
anything they pray for why don't Deacon Winn get
back the money he lost on pork? Why can't the
widow get back her silver snuff-box that was stole?
Why can't Miss Watson fat up? No, says I to myself,
there ain't nothin to it.[1]

In contrast to this view James wrote, "The effective prayer
of a righteous man can accomplish much. Elijah was a man with
a nature like ours, and he prayed earnestly that it might not
rain; and it did not rain on the earth for three years and six
months. And he prayed again, and the sky poured rain, and the
earth produced its fruit" (James 5:16b-18). Prayer, according to
James, can even affect even the weather!

## The Problem With Prayer

The purpose of this chapter is not to present ways to pray
more effectively. There are several good books which deal with
this aspect of our prayer life. We are more concerned about the
antinomy of prayer. The antinomy can be stated very simply: If
God is sovereign and is working out all things according to His
plan, what possible effect could my prayer life have on God's
will? On the other hand, if God is not sovereign, what use is there
in praying, since God cannot answer? Obviously, if man is given
no responsibility and free will, then prayer will accomplish nothing because God's will has already determined the outcome of
every event.

So here we have two facts, both of which are true and yet
seem to contradict each other.

1. God is sovereign. All things are being worked out according to His predetermined plan.

2. Man is responsible before God for his choice and is instructed through God's Word to pray about everything.

How can both facts be true? In chapter 6, I dealt with this antinomy in connection with man's freedom. In this chapter we shall consider how prayer can affect God's plan for His creation. I would suggest a re-reading of chapter 6 in order to be better prepared for the following thoughts on prayer.

## Prayer and Sovereignty

In order to understand how prayer can affect God's plan for His creation, we must understand that God exists outside the realm of time while at the same time He is able to operate within the framework of earth's time. The past, present, and future are all in the present with God. When God views an event in our past and another event in our future, both are in the "now" with Him. "Remember the former things long past, for I am God and there is no other, I am God, and there is no one like Me, declaring the end from the beginning and from ancient times things which have not been done, saying, 'My purpose will be established, and I will accomplish all My good pleasure' " (Isaiah 46:9, 10).

God is able to "declare the end from the beginning" because both appear simultaneously to Him. Once we have comprehended the fact that God does not move along a time line as we do with events that are in the past, present, and future, we'll be better able to understand how He can arrange events to accomplish His will. God is able to look at all events (past, present, future) that have taken place on earth in the lives of billions of people in one moment. There is nothing that surprises God or that "catches Him off guard." He saw every event before the world was created.

C. S. Lewis made the following insightful observation,

> Most of our prayers, if fully analyzed, ask either for a miracle or for events whose foundation will have to have been laid before I was born, indeed, laid

when the universe began. But then to God (though not to me) I and the prayer I make in 1945 were just as much present at the creation of the world as they are now and will be a million years hence. God's creative act is timeless and timelessly adapted to the "free" elements within it: but this timeless adaptation meets our consciousness as a sequence of prayer and answer.

Two corollaries follow:

1. People often ask whether a given event (not a miracle) was really an answer to prayer or not. I think that if they analyze their thought they will find they are asking, "Did God bring it about for a special purpose or would it have happened anyway as part of the natural course of events?" But this (like the old question, "Have you left off beating your wife?") makes either answer impossible. In the play Hamlet, Ophelia climbs out on a branch overhanging a river; the branch breaks, she falls in and drowns. What would you reply if anyone asked, "Did Ophelia die because Shakespeare for poetic reasons wanted her to die at that moment—or because the branch broke?" I think one would have to say, "For both reasons." Every event in the play happens as a result of other events in the play, but also every event happens because the poet wants it to happen. All events in the play are Shakespearian events; similarly all events in the world are providential events. All events in the play, however, come about (or ought to come about) by the dramatic logic of events. Similarly all events in the real world (except miracles) come about by natural causes. "Providence" and natural causation are not alternatives; both determine every event because both are one.

2. When we are praying about the result, say, of a battle or a medical consultation the thought will often cross our minds that (if only we knew it) the event is already decided one way or the other. I believe this to be no good reason for ceasing our

prayers. The event certainly has been decided—in a sense it was decided "before all worlds." But one of the things taken into account in deciding it, and therefore one of the things that really cause it to happen, may be this very prayer that we are now offering. Thus, shocking as it may sound, I conclude that we can at noon become part causes of an event occurring at ten o'clock.[2]

J. Oswald Sanders wrote, "Since God has commanded us to pray, prayer must form part of His overall purpose. Since He has pledged Himself to answer these prayers, is it not reasonable to assume that in His scheme of things He has made full allowance for all the implications of prayer? Could it not be that our prayers form part of His plan and purpose?"[3]

When this concept begins to dawn on you, the implications of it are staggering. Think about it for a moment. Suppose you pray about an event that is about to transpire in the future. You know that in a sense the outcome of that event has already been determined, but what is amazing is the fact that God can allow your prayer to enter into the event and He can arrange the event to fit the request of your prayer. What is still more amazing is that God did this before the "foundation of the world." That means that if you failed to pray about the event, the outcome could be very different.

When we pray in accordance to God's will, our prayers actually enter into His will and thus can determine the outcome of various events. Our free will contributes to the present and future events of this world, and that contribution was made before the world was created.

Paul wrote, "First of all, then I urge that entreaties and prayers, petitions and thanksgivings, be made on behalf of all men, for kings and all who are in authority, in order that we may lead a tranquil and quiet life in all godliness and dignity" (1 Timothy 2:1, 2). How could God answer a prayer like that without taking it into His will long before the prayer was actually uttered by the individual? Paul also suggests that if we don't pray for these things, the circumstances of our own lives will be quite different.

Lewis observes,

> The imagination will, no doubt, try to play all sorts of tricks on us at this point. It will ask, "Then if I stop praying can God go back and alter what has already happened?" No. The event has already happened and one of its causes is your present prayer. Thus something does really depend on my choice. My free act contributes to the cosmic shape. That contribution is made in eternity or "before all worlds"; but my consciousness of contributing reaches me at a particular point in the time series.[4]

With this insight into the power of prayer and the sovereignty of God, we can better understand Paul's admonition, "Be anxious for nothing, but in everything by prayer and supplication with thanksgiving let your requests be made known to God" (Philippians 4:6). The more we pray, the more we will see God working in our lives through answered prayer; therefore, the less anxious we'll be, knowing that God really does hear and answer our prayers.

## Unanswered Prayers

Every Christian has experienced times in which it seemed that prayer was ineffectual. With the psalmist we cry, "Do not hide Thy face from me, do not turn Thy servant away . . . do not abandon me nor forsake me" (Psalm 27:9). Job cried out, "Why dost Thou hide Thy face, and consider me Thine enemy?" (Job 13:24). At times it does seem that God has turned away. How do we explain this in light of the promises in God's Word that He does answer prayer? Quoting again from Lewis,

> The Christian is not to ask whether this or that event happened because of a prayer. He is rather to believe that all events without exception are answers to prayer in the sense that whether they are

grantings or refusals the prayers of all concerned and their needs have all been taken into account. All prayers are heard, though not all prayers are granted. We must not picture destiny as a film unrolling for the most part on its own in which our prayers are sometimes allowed to insert additional items. On the contrary, what the film displays to us as it unrolls already contains the results of our prayers and of all our other acts. There is no question whether an event has happened because of your prayer. When the event you prayed for occurs your prayer has always contributed to it. When the opposite event occurs your prayer has never been ignored; it has been considered and refused for your ultimate good and the good of the whole universe.[5]

This is illustrated in the life of the apostle Paul. He wrote:

And because of the surpassing greatness of the revelations, for this reason, to keep me from exalting myself, there was given me a thorn in the flesh, a messenger of Satan to buffet me—to keep me from exalting myself! Concerning this I entreated the Lord three times that it might depart from me. And He has said to me, "My grace is sufficient for you, for power is perfected in weakness." Most gladly, therefore, I will rather boast about my weakness, that the power of Christ may dwell in me. Therefore I am well content with weaknesses, with insults, with distresses, with persecutions, with difficulties, for Christ's sake; for when I am weak, then I am strong (2 Corinthians 12:7-10).

Note the benefits that came to Paul because of his prayer being denied.

1. Humility (it prevented self-exaltation).
2. Deeper appreciation of God's grace.
3. Greater dependency on God during weakness.

4. Greater realization of Christ's indwelling power.

5. Contentment in spite of circumstances.

In addition to the above, Paul has been an inspiration over the centuries to thousands of people as to how one may profit from unanswered prayer. What great joy the Christian has in knowing that every prayer worded before the throne of God will be considered by the sovereign God of the universe, and His infinite wisdom will provide the exact and proper answer for the well-being of all involved. It is with such understanding of prayer that Paul very simply stated, "Pray without ceasing" (1 Thessalonians 5:18).

## God's Sovereignty

Behavior is determined by belief. If a person believes that he is poor at mathematics, the outcome of a math test is almost predictable. If a young lady believes that she is the prettiest girl in school, her behavior will reflect the pride which she takes in her beauty.

If one believes that God has gone away on vacation after raising Christ from the dead and inspiring the Scriptures, then one's life will reflect a belief in self-preservation and self-achievement. On the other hand, if one believes in the sovereignty of God, one's life will reflect a trust in God's love and in God's power of preservation and control.

Faith in God's sovereignty is of utmost importance in order to turn over the control of our lives to Him. We must believe that He cares. "Casting all your anxiety upon Him, because He cares for you" (1 Peter 5:7). J. B. Phillips translated this text beautifully, "You can throw the whole weight of your anxieties upon Him, for you are His personal concern."

Prayer should be the Christian's "vital breath" because he knows that God has allowed him to have a "voice" in the operation, control, and direction of the created order. What grand privileges prayer affords the Christian! No wonder Jesus said that we "ought to pray and not to lose heart" (Luke 18:1).

## Notes

[1]Mark Twain, *The Adventures of Huckleberry Finn* (New York: Harper and Brothers, 1896), p. 15.

[2]C. S. Lewis, *Miracles* (New York: The Macmillan Company, 1947), pp. 376-377.

[3]J. Oswald Sanders, *Prayer Power Unlimited* (Chicago, IL: The Moody Bible Institute, 1977), p. 101.

[4]Lewis, pp. 377-378.

[5]Ibid., pp. 378-379.

## Remembering the Facts

1. How does prayer present an antinomy to the human mind?

2. When God views an event in our past and another event in our future, both are in the _____ with Him.

3. Why do most of our prayers ask either for a miracle or for changes in events already settled?

4. What is one of the things that God takes into account in deciding the outcome of events in our lives?

5. When we pray in accordance to God's will, our prayers actually enter into His_____.

6. How is 1 Timothy 2:1 an example of God answering a prayer before it is actually verbalized?

7. How should a Christian view all events in the world?

8. List the five benefits that came to Paul as a result of his prayer being denied:

    (1)

    (2)

    (3)

    (4)

    (5)

9. What was Paul's instruction on prayer in 1 Thessalonians 5:18?

10. How can our faith in God's sovereignty strengthen our prayer life?

## Discussing the Issues

1. What is the most difficult thing for you to believe about prayer?

2. What are some of the problems that you have observed (if any) about public prayers in church? How or why have these problems developed?

3. Do you believe it is right to direct a thought to God in prayer at any given moment without using the phrase "In Jesus' name, Amen"?

4. What does it mean to "pray in faith"?

# Chapter 9
# Spiritual Maturity—God's Power or Man's Effort?

> . . . work out your own salvation with fear and trembling; . . . (Philippians 2:12).
>
> . . . for it is God who is at work in you, both to will and to work for His good pleasure (Philippians 2:13).

I am convinced that the area in which most Christians experience their greatest difficulty is that of understanding what spiritual maturity is all about. The list of things which people use to gauge maturity is almost endless. A few of them are Bible knowledge, generous giving, faithful attendance at all services, soul winning or personal evangelism, participation in work programs and church committees, refraining from certain sins (e.g., lying, cursing, immorality), exercising spiritual gifts, regular prayer times, etc.

Almost every Christian has a list of dos and don'ts which comprise a definition of maturity. It is believed by most people that if the "list" is followed closely and carefully, the individual will be pleasing to God and will be found faithful in the end.

## Origin of the Confusion

The confusion over what constitutes spiritual maturity actually goes back to one's understanding of salvation. A misunderstanding concerning salvation will inevitably lead to a misunderstanding of how one grows and develops in the Lord. If salvation is viewed as totally man's effort, apart from grace, then maturity will also be gauged by effort and works. On the other hand, if one views salvation as totally God's work, then maturity will be totally dependent on God's role in the Christian's life. Either extreme in this antinomy can lead to a disastrous and miserable Christian existence. Finding the balance in this antinomy will bring great peace and satisfaction to the Christian.

In order to clear up some of the confusion over the subject of maturity, it would be helpful to have a clear understanding of justification and sanctification. The words "just," "justify," and "justification" are used in both the Old Testament and New Testament to refer to relationships. When a person is justified, he is made right either with his fellow man or with God. A person who has been justified with God has been reconciled to God, that is, the individual has been set right with God. This is a process which only God can accomplish. The fact that man cannot justify himself with God is made clear in both testaments (Psalm 143:2; Job 25:4; Isaiah 57:12; 64:6; Acts 13:39; Galatians 2:16). Justification is a judicial act by which God declares a person to be righteous on the basis of Christ's atonement.

The terms "sanctify" and "sanctification" imply the making of something (i.e., a process complete or incomplete), but not in any event the finished product itself. The term "sanctify" carries the idea of holiness. To be sanctified means to be in the process of becoming holy. In the Greek, the words "sanctify" and "holy" actually come from the same root word.[1]

Sanctification is pictured in the New Testament as a process that is both completed and at the same time in the process of being completed. "But you were sanctified, but you were justified in the name of the Lord Jesus, and in the Spirit of our God" (1 Corinthians 6:11). "But we should always give thanks to God for you, brethren beloved of the Lord, because God has chosen you from the beginning for salvation through sanctification by the Spirit and faith in the truth" (2 Thessalonians 2:13). "Who are chosen according to the foreknowledge of God the Father, by the sanctifying work of the Spirit" (1 Peter 1:2).

Several passages present sanctification as a goal to strive for in the Christian experience. "Therefore, having these promises, beloved, let us cleanse ourselves from all defilement of flesh and spirit, perfecting holiness in the fear of God" (2 Corinthians 7:1).

"For this is the will of God, your sanctification; that is, that you abstain from sexual immorality" (1 Thessalonians 4:3). "Present your members as slaves to righteousness, resulting in sanctification" (Romans 6:19).

The temptation has been for Bible students to define justification as a past experience and sanctification as a present, ongoing experience toward a life of perfection or holiness. This, plus a confusion over salvation by grace, has led to a total misunderstanding of what constitutes maturity in Christian living. Thus there are two serious errors that many people hold concerning sanctification:

1. That it is a process separate from justification.
2. That it is a process by which one secures salvation.

## Sanctification and Justification

Figure 5 illustrates the common view of man's salvation in three phases. You will note that justification is viewed as a one-time experience in the past by which all previous sins committed up to that point are forgiven. From that point on, the process of sanctification will determine a person's eternal destiny. If one grows in obedience, love, and faith, one will please God and receive an eternal reward. If the process of sanctification ceases, the person's spiritual life dies and eternal reward is lost.

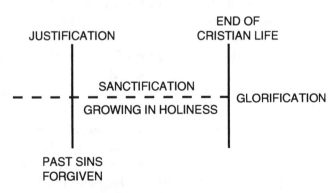

*Figure No. 5*

As you can see, the whole process of one's eternal salvation is dependent not on justification but rather on sanctification. Justification becomes subordinate to sanctification. This concept is what produces the religious mentality that describes spiritual maturity in terms mentioned in paragraph one of this chapter (i.e., Bible knowledge, generous giving, et al.). This concept also provides an abundance of material for preachers who brow-beat their people into frenzied activity out of fear that a failure to do these things would jeopardize their eternal salvation.

Eventually the fruit of this theology will be seen in the lives of neurotic Christians who immerse themselves in endless rounds of activities (many of which they disdain) in hopes of being found faithful in the end. They will have lost the joy of salvation, if indeed they ever possessed it, and much of their energy will be expended in activities that have very little value insofar as true spiritual growth is concerned. Their spiritual maturity will be measured in terms of outward values such as attendance at service, Bible verses memorized, committees chaired, classes taught, conversions, etc. Once an individual begins to excel in one or more areas, it then is very tempting to look down on those who have not achieved this status. The pharisaical mentality begins to take over. When a person eventually reaches a place where service is no longer possible because of poor health or aging, the process of sanctification comes to an end. Salvation then comes into jeopardy.

There are many Christians who have been in the church for years who have given themselves totally to the Lord's work and are now unable to serve as they once did. They live in fear and uncertainty because the process of sanctification, as they understand it, has virtually ceased. Many of these will face death with no secure hope of eternal salvation. At a time when their hope should be the strongest and their assurance of salvation beyond doubt, they find themselves living in fear and torment.

Figure 6 illustrates the biblical view of justification and sanctification. Justification must always be the over-arching principle of salvation. The Christian must always look out from himself to the cross of Christ for his forgiveness. His faith must center in on the righteousness of Christ instead of his own righteousness. He must see himself with the eye of faith, as God sees him—clothed in the righteousness of Christ. His life is "hidden with Christ in God" (Colossians 3:3).

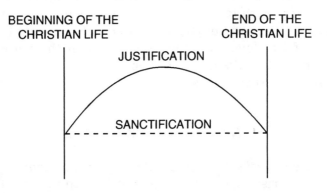

BEGINNING OF THE
CHRISTIAN LIFE

END OF THE
CHRISTIAN LIFE

JUSTIFICATION

SANCTIFICATION

*Figure No. 6*

The Christian receives the cleansing of Christ's atonement continually as he grows in his sanctification. "If we walk in the light as He Himself is in the light, we have fellowship with one another, and the blood of Jesus His Son cleanses us from all sin" (1 John 1:7). The verb "cleanses" is a present tense verb in the Greek, which suggests a continuous cleansing action. As the Christian grows in his sanctification (walking in the light) he must depend on the ever-present, continuous cleansing of Christ's blood, because there will always be sins that need to be confessed (1 John 1:8, 9). Sanctification and justification are not two separate actions occurring at different times, but both are part of the process of salvation. J. K. S. Reid wrote,

> It is tempting for the sake of logical neatness to make a clear division between the two (sanctification and justification, B.R.S.); but the temptation must be resisted, if in fact the division is absent from Holy Scripture. The definition of terms at this point is eased if justification be given a declaratory, imputed or forensic character. The way is then open to regarding sanctification as the real status thereby conferred, which in its turn awaits exemplification,

practice or exercise, just as from the newly accoladed nobleman one expects noble deeds.[2]

The proper concept of sanctification, therefore, is to see it as a process of growth toward maturity in response to the justification that one already enjoys in Christ's atonement. It is a response of faith, love, and obedience through the power of the Holy Spirit to the blessing of redemption that one receives on a continual basis from Jesus Christ.

## A New Testament Concept

The New Testament principle of sanctification is one in which the Christian is admonished to live up to his calling. "I, therefore, the prisoner of the Lord, entreat you to walk in a manner worthy of the calling with which you have been called . . ." (Ephesians 4:1). Paul is admonishing duty as a response to doctrine. The link between the two is the word "therefore," which means "as a result of what you have received in Christ, here is what you are to do." This pattern is found in almost all of Paul's epistles. Here are some examples:

> I urge you therefore, brethren, by the mercies of God, to present your bodies a living and holy sacrifice, acceptable to God, which is your spiritual service of worship (Romans 12:1; 11 chapters of doctrine, 5 chapters of duty).

> It was for freedom that Christ set us free; therefore, keep standing firm and do not be subject again to a yoke of slavery (Galatians 5:1; 4 chapters of doctrine, 2 chapters of duty).

You will note that the word "therefore" bridges doctrine and duty or justification and sanctification. Sanctification is an outgrowth of justification.

A good illustration of this principle is the framing of a formal resolution. The first item is the preamble—"whereas a certain situation exists, or whereas we hold certain convictions . . ."

Next comes the formal resolution—"Therefore be it resolved that certain action will be taken . . ." The order is very important—first is the preamble then the resolution. The resolution never comes before the preamble, and the preamble is of little value without the resolution.

In the New Testament, the Christian is told what the preamble is and then he is encouraged to live the resolution. Spiritual maturity is learning to live up to our calling, or in other words, making our experience equal to our judicial position. The following chart illustrates this principle.[3] You will note that with every preamble (doctrine) there is a corresponding resolution (duty).

| **Preamble** **What God Has Done** | **Resolution** **What we have to Do** |
|---|---|
| (2 Peter 1:3, 4; Ephesians 1:3; Colossians 2:10; Hebrews 10:14) | (2 Peter 1:5-8; Ephesians 4:1; 2 Timothy 3:17; Colossians 4:12; Hebrews 13:20, 21) |
| *Alive to God* (Ephesians 2:1, 4, 5; 1 John 4:9 John 11:25; 14:19) | *Live for God* (Philippians 1:21; Galatians 2:20; Romans 6:11-13; Titus 2:12) |
| *Freed from sin* (Ephesians 1:7, 1 John 1:9; 2:12; Romans 6:2-10) | *Don't give in to sin* (Romans 6:11-15; Colossians 3:3) |
| *Forgiven of all sin* (Ephesians 1:7; 1 John 1:9; 2:12; Colossians 1:14) | *Live as a forgiven person* (Romans 8:1, 2, 33, 34) |
| *Declared righteous* (Romans 3:21-26; 4:1, 6; 5:17) | *Live a righteous life* (2 Timothy 2:22; 1 John 3:7) |
| *Sons of God* (Ephesians 1:5; Galatians 3:26 | *Live God's sons* (Ephesians 5:1; 1 Peter 1:13, 14) |
| *God's possession* (2 Timothy 2:19) | *Give yourself to God* (Romans 12:1; 2 Timothy 2:19-21) |
| *Heirs of God/fellow heirs with Christ* (Romans 8:17; Colossians 1:12; Ephesians 1:11, 14, 18; 1 Peter 1:3, 4) | *Add to your inheritance* (Matthew 6:19-21; 2 Corinthians 5:9, 10; 2 John 8; 1 Corinthians 3:12-14 |

| | |
|---|---|
| Blessed with every spiritual blessing in the heavenly places in Christ<br>(Ephesians 1:3; 2:6, 7) | Keep your mind on your position<br>(Colossians 3:1, 2 |
| Citizenship in heaven<br>(Philippians 3:20; 1 John 5:4, 5) | Live as an alien on earth<br>(1 John 2:15; Colossians 3:1, 2; James 1:27) |
| Slave<br>(1 Corinthians 7:22, 23; Romans 8:22) | Be a slave to righteousness<br>(Romans 6:17-19; 12:11; Hebrews 12:28) |
| New creation in Christ<br>(2 Corinthians 5:17) | Walk in newness of life<br>(Romans 6:4) |
| No longer under law<br>(Romans 6:14; 7:1-6) | Fulfull the requirements of the law<br>(Romans 8:4) |
| Delivered from present evil age<br>(Galatians 1:4; 6:14) | Don't love the world<br>(1 John 2:15-17; James 4:4; Romans 12:2) |
| Sons of light to the world<br>(1 Thessalonians 5:5; Matthew 5:14) | Let your light shine<br>(Matthew 5:15, 16) |
| Power over Satan through Christ's blood<br>(Revelation 12:9-11) | Stand firm against Satan<br>(Ephesians 6:11-17; James 4:7) |
| Cleansed by Christ's blood<br>(John 15:3; 1 John 1:7, 9) | Stay Clean!<br>(2 Corinthians 7:1) |
| Holy and blameless before God<br>(Ephesians 1:4; 1 Corinthians 3:17) | Live holy and blameless lives<br>(1 Peter 1:15, 16; 2 Peter 3:14) |
| Freed by the truth<br>(John 8:32) | Stand firm in your freedom<br>(Galatians 5:1) |
| Placed in Christ judicially<br>(Ephesians 1:3, 10; 2:6, 13) | Abide in Him experientially<br>(1 John 2:28) |
| Protected by the power of God<br>(1 Peter 1:5; Romans 8) | Live a secure life<br>(2 Peter 1:10, 11) |
| At peace with God<br>(Romans 5:1; 14:17; John 14:27; Acts 10:36) | Pursue things that produce peace<br>(Romans 14:19; Colossians 3:15; 2 Timothy 2:22; 1 Thessalonians 5:13) |

*In one body—the church*
(Ephesians 4:4-6; 1 Corinthians 12:13)

*Live in unity (oneness) with the church*
(Ephesians 4:3; John 17:21, 24)

*In God's grace*
(Romans 5:1, 2; Ephesians 2:8, 9, 10)

*Grow in grace and knowledge*
(2 Peter 3:18)

*In fellowship with God*
(1 John 1:3-7)

*Don't participate in deeds of darkness*
(1 Corinthians 10:20, 21; Ephesians 5:11)

*Joyful in hope of glory*
(Romans 5:2, 3)

*Make your joy complete*
(1 John 1:4; John 15:11; 16:24; Philippians 4:4)

*Your body is a temple of the Holy Spirit*
(1 Corinthians 6:19, 20; Romans 8:9, 14)

*Do not grieve or quench the Spirit*
(Ephesians 4:30; 5:18; 1 Thessalonians 5:19; Galatians 5:25)

*God has given you special gifts*
(1 Corinthians 12:4; Romans 12:6)

*Use your gifts to God's glory*
(Romans 12:3-6; 1 Peter 4:11)

*God's Power within you*
(Ephesians 3:20; 2 Corinthians 4:7; 2 Timothy 1:7)

*Live in the power of God's strength*
(1 Corinthians 2:4; Philippines 3:10; 4:13; Ephesians 6:10)

*Loved by God*
(Romans 5:5; 1 John 2:5)

*Love others*
(1 Peter 1:22; 4:8; John 13:34, 35; 1 John 3:18)

## Possessing Our Possessions

In order to be mature in the Christian life one must, in the words of Dr. Francis Schaeffer, "possess his possessions."4 A mature Christian responds lovingly and obediently to God's direction because God has blessed him so abundantly in Christ Jesus. He serves out of desire. Obedience is a matter of "want to," not "have to."

The goal of the Christian's experience is to live a life that reflects the exalted position which is attained in Christ Jesus. Watchman Nee writes, "What is the secret of the Christian life?

Whence has its power? Let me give you the answer in a sentence: *The Christian's secret is his rest in Christ*. His power derives from his God-given position."[5]

The power of sin is broken in the Christian's life, not through a teeth gritting determination to stop sinning, but rather from a realization that God has already declared the Christian dead to sin and has raised him up to sit in an exalted position in Christ at God's right hand. "Even so consider yourselves to be dead to sin, but alive to God in Christ Jesus" (Romans 6:11). "But God . . . made us alive together with Christ (by grace—you have been saved) and raised us up with Him, and seated us with Him in the heavenly places, in Christ Jesus" (Ephesians 2:6).

John R. W. Stott observes,

> Our biography is written in two volumes. Volume one is the story of the old man, the old self, of me before my conversion. Volume two is the story of the new man, the new self, of me after I was made a new creation in Christ. Volume one of my biography ended with the judicial death of the old self. I was a sinner. I deserved to die. I received my desserts in my Substitute with whom I have become one. Volume two of my biography opened with my resurrection. My old life having finished, a new life to God has begun. . . . Volume one has closed. You are now living in volume two. It is inconceivable that you should reopen volume one. It is not impossible, but it is inconceivable.[6]

## God's Power Man's Effort

Spiritual maturity is an antinomy. It is impossible without God's power, yet man must be willing to appropriate God's truth, by faith, into his life. It is important to keep the balance. If a person tries to mature through his own strength and will, the power of sin, through the law, will take over and control him (1 Corinthians 15:56). On the other hand, if one depends on God to produce maturity apart from yielding to the Spirit's leading, failure and disappointment will be the results.

In every Christian's life, there is the strain between the "already" and "not yet." Paul wrote in Philippians 3:12, "Not that I have already obtained it, or have already become perfect, but I press on in order that I may lay hold of that for which also I was laid hold of by Christ Jesus." The Hebrew writer declared in 10:14, "For by one offering He has perfected for all time those who are sanctified." So one writer declares that perfection has not been obtained, and another says that it has. How do we reconcile these two verses? Of course the answer is: there is no contradiction. In the Hebrew text, the writer declares that God "has perfected . . . those who are sanctified." The phrase "are sanctified" is in the present tense in Greek, which means continuous action. So the meaning of this verse is that the Christian is made perfect in Christ Jesus while in the process of being made perfect in the flesh (through sanctification).

Miles Stanford sums up beautifully the proper attitude of the mature believer. "Our position as new creations is not in this sin-cursed world. We are traveling through it, but not abiding in it. How is it that the growing believer can rest and be at peace in the midst of death, free to hold forth and share the Word of life? It is simply because his anchorage and source of life is in another person in another world."[7]

What great joy to live a life to God's glory, learning moment by moment how to reflect that glory in daily experience. The Christian life at times will be difficult, certainly challenging, and sometimes discouraging, but it can never be boring, dull, or routine. Every day is a glorious opportunity to learn something new about our exalted position in Christ. With that new knowledge we can grow more into the image of Christ as we continue to "reign in life through the One, Jesus Christ" (Romans 5:17).

## Notes

[1]J. K. S. Reid, "Sanctification," in Alan Richardson (ed.), *A Theological Word Book of the Bible* (New York: The Macmillan Co., 1950), p.216.

[2]Ibid., pp. 218-219.

[3]Revised from John MacArthurs *Body Dynamics* (Wheaton, IL: Victor Books, 1982), pp. 45-48.

[4]Francis A. Schaeffer, *True Sprituality* (Wheaton, IL: Tyndale House Publishers, 1971), p. 84.

[5]Watchman Nee, *Sit, Walk, Stand* (Fort Washington, PA: Christian Literature Crusade, 1957), p. 28.

[6]John R. W. Stott, *Man Made New* (Downers Grove, IL: Inter Varsity Press, 1966), pp. 49-50.

[7]Miles J. Stanford, *The Ground of Growth* (Grand Rapids, MI: Zondervan Publishing House, 1976), p. 76.

## Remembering the Facts

1. The words "just," "justify," and "justification" are used in the Old and New Testaments to refer to relationships. What is significant about this term in connection with our relationship to God?

2. What is the meaning of sanctification?

3. What is the one serious mistake that most Bible students make in defining justification and sanctification?

4. The proper concept of sanctification is to see it as a process of growth toward maturity. It must always be a response to what?

5. The link between doctrine and duty is found in a "bridge" word used often in the New Testament. What is that word?

6. Spiritual maturity involves two principles, reflected in the terms preamble and resolution. Define what each means in connection with spiritual growth:

   Preamble:

   Resolution:

7. Obedience must be a matter of "want to," not what?

8. What should be the goal of the Christian's life?

9. How does the Christian break the power of sin in his life?

10. What happens when a person tries to mature in his own strength?

## Discussing the Issues

1. Why is the Christian's identity with Christ "in heavenly places" so important to his self-image?

2. How can confusion on the subject of salvation lead to greater confusion about spiritual maturity?

3. What attitude and reaction should the mature Christian take toward those who misunderstand what maturity is all about and endeavor to squeeze others into their mold?

4. Can pride be a problem for the mature Christian? Why or why not?

# Chapter 10
# Salvation—Secure or Conditional?

> Now to Him who is able to keep you from stumbling, and to make you stand in the presence of His glory . . . (Jude 24).
>
> Therefore let him who thinks he stands take heed lest he fall (1 Corinthians 10:12).

Of all the biblical antinomies, there are no two that are more clear-cut than the subjects of this chapter. The line that has been drawn between these two issues is "hard and fast." There seems to be very little conciliation on either side. It is almost an either/or, cut-and-dried fact: either salvation is eternally secure and can never be jeopardized in any way or salvation is conditional and may be forfeited at any moment.

John Calvin . . . Jacob Arminius. These are the men primarily responsible for the great division that exists on these issues. Calvin believed that the substitutionary death of Jesus Christ was intended to save the elect only. Those sovereignly elected to salvation would never resist God's grace nor would they ever lose their salvation. They would be kept by God's power unto eternal life. Arminius took the opposite view—stating that salvation was received conditionally (i.e., on the basis of free will) and thus could also be forfeited on the same basis. So the debate has continued.

## Evidence of Salvation

In order to better understand this antinomy, the question that needs to be asked and answered is: How does one know for sure that he has eternal life? Paul wrote, "The Spirit Himself bears witness with our spirit that we are children of God" (Romans 8:16). This verse teaches that a Christian can know whether he/she possesses eternal life. However, this verse has been a center of controversy. Some believe that the evidence of sonship is purely subjective—that is, one can know through feelings, emotions, or an "inner witness" that one possesses eternal life. Others interpret this verse to mean that the Spirit has given witness in the Word of God as to what a child of God is, and when a person's life, faith, love, and obedience match the Spirit's description, that is evidence of sonship.

The question of assurance is an important one for both the Calvinistic and Arminian positions. It is also one that both groups have struggled with at length.

Dr. Lewis Sperry Chafer wrote, "Adherents to eternal security agree that a person can experience a superficial conversion or outward change in his life, may go through the outer motions of accepting Christ such as joining a church or being baptized, and even experience a measure of change in his life pattern, yet still be short of real salvation in Christ."[1] If Chafer is correct, the question arises: How can a person know if the conversion experience is real or superficial?

Calvin struggled with these issues. He believed that the elect could have the assurance of salvation based on the inner witness of the Spirit. However, he also believed that the non-elect could receive a similar inner witness, even to the extent that the non-elect would actually believe that they were among the elect.

Calvin wrote: "Experience shows that the reprobate are sometimes affected in a way so similar to the elect that, even in their own judgment, there is no difference between them."[2] Proponents of Calvinism are quick to say that the superficial believer will eventually give up the faith and return to sin. But they will also admit that a true believer (i.e., one of the elect) may also drift away. However, the true believer will never lose eternal life.

It is obvious to the thinking person that the doctrine of eternal security as illustrated by the above is not one that actually produces security in the believer. Here is why. Let's suppose that a man decides to become a Christian; he begins to study God's Word, puts his trust in Christ, and turns from his evil ways, committing his life to Christ. How does he know for sure that he is saved eternally? The Calvinist will answer, "Because he has the 'inner witness.' " But how does he know for sure that the witness is true? The Arminian will answer that he cannot know absolutely beyond any doubt that he is saved eternally because he may later turn away and lose his salvation.

If the person later turns away from Christ, the Calvinist will point to that as evidence that the person's faith was never true and that he was not one of the elect. However, there is a problem here because the Calvinist must also admit that it is possible for one of the elect to also turn away. Chafer wrote, "A genuine Christian may also lose his fellowship with God because of sin . . . and be deprived of some of the present benefits of being saved such as having the fruit of the Spirit . . . and enjoying the satisfaction of effective service for Christ."[3]

Think for a moment—if this man falls away, he will assume that he was never one of the elect and so give up completely. Or he may conclude that he is one of the elect, but has temporarily drifted away; nevertheless, he has not lost his salvation, so he will not be too concerned about his condition. In either case there is great confusion here. The point is—one can never *really* know for sure if one is saved eternally or not. This is true because Calvin finally concluded that the ultimate ground of assurance of one's election is deliberate perseverance in faith. However, one can never be absolutely sure that he/she will persevere to the end; tomorrow may bring apostasy. But if one apostatizes, that cannot be absolute proof of one's non-election or election. Sound confusing? It is!

It has been pointed out by scholars that superficial believers are not the only type that fall away. In Luke 8:9-15 Jesus gave the Parable of the Sower. Four groups of people are described in this text. One group hears the Word of God without believing it. A second group "believe for a while, and in time of temptation fall away" (Luke 8:13). A. T. Robertson comments: "Ostensibly they are sincere and have a real start in the life of faith."[4]

The next group of believers, described as the "thorny ground," are the ones "who have heard, and as they go on their way they are choked with worries and riches and pleasures of this life, and bring no fruit to maturity" (verse 14). The fourth group "are the ones who have heard the word in an honest and good heart, and hold it fast, and bear fruit with perseverance" (verse 15).

The apostle Paul apparently realized that even though sincere, he could depart from the ministry. "I buffet my body and make it my slave, lest possibly, after I have preached to others, I myself should be disqualified" (1 Corinthians 9:27). A. T. Robertson has this observation: "Most writers take Paul to refer to the possibility of his rejection in his personal salvation at the end of the race ... It is a humbling thought for us all to see this wholesome fear instead of smug complacency in this greatest of all heralds of Christ (cf. 1 Cor. 8:11; 10:12)."[5] The reference of Robertson to 1 Corinthians 10:12 has the warning, "Therefore let him who thinks he stands take heed lest he fall." Whether Paul is speaking of eternal life or the loss of His own ministry could be debated. However, the Bible does teach us there is some personal responsibility to remain close to Christ in our daily walk. But while we realize these personal warnings are real, we must also realize that we do not have the strength within ourselves to live the Christian life apart from God's election of us and the indwelling of His Holy Spirit. Herein lies the balance in this difficult antinomy.

## Secure in Christ

The subject of election and eternal security is of vital importance. Paul makes it very clear that eternal security and divine election as well as predestination and foreknowledge are all in Christ, the Chosen One. "Blessed be the God and Father of our Lord Jesus Christ, who has blessed us with every spiritual blessing in the heavenly places in Christ, just as He chose us in Him before the foundation of the world, that we should be holy and blameless before Him. In love He predestined us to adoption as sons through Jesus Christ to Himself, according to the kind intention of His will, to the praise of the glory of His grace, which He freely bestowed on us in the Beloved" (Ephesians 1:3-6).

There is no question that God chooses in Christ those who are to receive eternal life. The reason for His choosing the elect is that they are incapable of making the right choices themselves. Jeremiah's commentary on human nature is, "The heart is . . . desperately wicked; Who can know it?" (Jeremiah 17:9).

Michael Horton has observed:

> If the will is no more than an expression of character, it will never choose something contrary to the character of the chooser. Hence, our Lord's remark to the Pharisees, "You are not *able* to listen to My word. You are of your father the devil, and the desires of your father you want to do" (John 8:43-44). Because they are *of* their father the devil, it follows that their *desires* are his desires. And notice He said, "the desires of your father *you want to do*." You really *want* to obey the one to whom you are bound. That is the point. If God left you to yourself, to decide whether you would choose Him or reject Him, you would always refuse God as long as you are "of your father the devil." As long as you are a child of Adam, Jesus said, "You are not able to listen to My word" (verse 43). Your will always follows your character, your heart, your affections.

> We often practice our evangelism as though gimmicks and techniques could get people to raise a hand or walk an aisle or pray a prayer. Sometimes such methods do get people to do these things, but that is not regeneration or conversion. We have simply gotten them to jump through our hoops. Essentially, election is God's making the decision for us that we would never have made for Him. "In this is love, not that we loved (or chose) God, but that He loved (and chose) us" (1 John 4:10). When we choose God, it costs us nothing, compared to the cost of His choosing us.

> But when a person does *will* to come, it is because he or she has been chosen and converted by God's grace alone. Hence, when a person does come it is, as

far as that person is concerned, a free choice, because no one externally coerced the choice. God changes our natural, self-oriented disposition and frees us for the first time from bondage to our sinful will, and then we make the decision that is in harmony with our new, regenerated nature.[6]

## Assurance of Eternal Lite

The assurance of eternal life is based on the knowledge of one's relationship with Christ. It is not some inner voice that tells one that salvation is secure, but rather an understanding that eternal life is in the Son of God. So John wrote, "These things I have written to you who believe in the name of the Son of God, in order that you may know that you have eternal life" (1 John 5:13).

Eternal life is the life of God that one enjoys as one follows Jesus Christ. As long as faith remains in Christ, eternal life is absolutely secure and cannot be lost. "Here is the perseverance of the saints who keep the commandments of God and their faith in Jesus" (Revelation 14:12). But don't fear that you will fail because "He . . . is able to keep you from stumbling, and to make you stand in the presence of His glory . . ."(Jude 24).

Phillip Schaff summed up the conflict between these two major theological conflicts when he wrote, "The Bible gives us a theology which is more human than Calvinism, and more divine than Arminianism, and more Christian than either of them."[7] This is usually the case with most of the conflicts that man finds in the Holy Scripture. It is of utmost importance to read the Bible carefully and reverently, avoiding the inevitable temptation of going off into extremes with the biblical antinomies. Maintaining such a balance as to understand and appreciate *all* biblical truth will bring much joy and consolation as one grows in the "grace and knowledge of our Lord Jesus Christ."

## Notes

[1]Lewis Sperry Chafer, *Major Bible Themes*, Revised by John F. Walvoord (Grand Rapids, MI: Zondervan Publishers, 1970), p. 211.

[2]Quoted by Robert Shank, *Elect in the Son—A Study of the Doctrine of Election* (Springfield, MO: Westcott Publishers, 1970), p. 211.

[3]Chafer, p. 222.

[4]A. T. Robertson, *Word Pictures in the New Testament* (Nashville: Sunday School Board of the Southern Baptist Convention, 1930), Vol. II, p. 114.

[5]Ibid., Vol. IV, p. 150.

[6]Michael Scott Horton, *Putting Amazing Back Into Grace, An Introduction to Reformed Theology* (Nashville, TN: Thomas Nelson Publishers, 1991), pp. 44-45.

[7]Philip Schaff, *History of the Christian Church* (Grand Rapids, MI: Wm. B. Eerdmans Publishing Co., 1882-1910), Vol. VIII, p. 816.

## Remembering the Facts

1. Who are the two men who were primarily responsible for the two extreme positions (Calvinism and Arminianism) which are prominent today in the antinomy of salvation?

2. On what basis did John Calvin believe that the elect could have assurance of salvation?

3. Explain why the following statement is true: "The doctrine of eternal security, as taught by Calvinism, is not one that actually produces security in the believer."

4. According to Ephesians 1:3-6, eternal security and divine election are found where?

5. What is eternal life?

6. How may one have assurance of eternal life?

## Discussing the Issues

1. How confident should a Christian be regarding his eternal salvation?

2. What role does fear play in a Christian's life? Can a Christian be too fearful of losing salvation?

# Chapter 11
# Resurrected Body—
# Spiritual or Material?

> . . . it is sown a natural body, it is raised a spiritual
> body (1 Corinthians 15:44).

> See My hands and My feet, that it is I Myself; touch
> Me and see, for a spirit does not have flesh and bones
> as you see that I have (Luke 24:39).

"But someone will say, 'How are the dead raised? And with
what kind of body do they come?' " Paul called this a fool's
question (1 Corinthians 15:35, 36a). The Greek word for "fool"
means "senseless one." Paul considers the question concerning
the kind of body one will have at the resurrection a foolish
inquiry into a subject that has no human answers. The reason
this is true is that the Bible presents the resurrection as an
antinomy. There are passages that support a physical resurrection of the body (e.g., Isaiah 26:19) and other passages that
support a spiritual resurrection (e.g., 1 Corinthians 15:44).

As is true with all the antinomies of Scripture, we must avoid
extremes. One could gather a number of passages that support a
material or physical resurrection while another could deny this
concept with texts that indicate a spiritual resurrection.

In order to ascertain the biblical truth on this antinomy, we
shall first study what the Bible says about Christ's resurrection
and then we'll see how our own resurrection will be like His.

## The Cornerstone

The resurrection of Jesus Christ is the cornerstone of Christianity. Without the resurrection all the subjects we are studying in this book are valueless (i.e., the deity of Christ, the Trinity, salvation, grace, sovereignty, eternal life, and faith). The grave is the only goal we have in life if Christ is not raised. The hope of every Christian centers on His promise, "Because I live, you shall live also" (John 14:19). John MacArthur Jr. observed, "It was this belief that turned the heartbroken followers of a crucified rabbi into the courageous martyrs of the early church."[1]

C. F. Evans wrote, "To a greater extent than it is anything else, Christianity—at least the Christianity of the New Testament—is a religion of resurrection."[2]

Dr. J. N. D. Anderson, professor of oriental law and the director of the Institute of Advanced Legal Studies at the University of London, did a great deal of research on the validity of Christ's resurrection. He observed, "It seems to me inescapable that anyone who chanced to read the pages of the New Testament for the first time would come away with one overwhelming impression, that there is a faith firmly rooted in certain allegedly historical events, a faith which would be false and misleading if those events had not actually taken place, but which—if they did take place—is unique in its relevance and exclusive in its demands on our allegiance."[3]

The most profound message of the New Testament is that Christ has been raised from the dead. The resurrection is mentioned 104 times in the New Testament. The first "good news" sermon about Jesus Christ was built around the resurrection. "This Jesus God raised up again, to which we are all witnesses" (Acts 2:32). Every sermon recorded in the book of Acts centers around the historical fact of the resurrection. As a matter of fact, the New Testament proclaims salvation predicated on belief in the resurrection. "If you confess with your mouth Jesus as Lord, and *believe in your heart that God raised Him from the dead*, you shall be saved" (Romans 10:9; emphasis added).

## The Hope of the Old Testament

As long as man has believed in the one true God, there has been hope for life after death. The book of Job is one of the oldest books in the Bible. Job's concept of a bodily resurrection from the dead is apparent in chapter 14:14, 15, "If a man dies, will he live again? All the days of my struggle I will wait until my change comes. Thou wilt call, and I will answer Thee; Thou wilt long for the work of Thy hands." Then in chapter 19 Job spoke of his resurrection when his Redeemer comes in the latter day: "And as for me, I know that my Redeemer lives, and at the last He will take His stand on the earth. Even after my skin is flayed, yet from my flesh I shall see God; whom I myself shall behold, and whom my eyes shall see and not another" (verses 25-27).

The term "from my flesh" indicates that Job believed in a bodily resurrection. The translators of the American Standard Version translated the Hebrew word "mibbesari" as "without my flesh." This is an unfortunate translation of the text; however, they did note in the marginal reading the correct translation "from my flesh." What Job literally said was, "Even after my skin (so diseased) is destroyed (referring to the body), yet from (the vantage point of) my flesh I shall see God." Then in verse 27 he says, "Whom my eyes shall see." In other words Job says, "I shall see God with my own physical eyes!"

What is amazing about the Old Testament's presentation of a bodily resurrection is that during the same time, contemporaneous heathen religions were permeated with fantastic ideas of a future life. The writers of the Old Testament retained a simple faith in God and in the resurrection of the dead without being influenced by heathen concepts.

This same concept of a material resurrection is brought over into the New Testament. Paul's letter to the Corinthians is the most extended treatment of the resurrection in the Bible.

## The Corinthian Confusion

The Corinthian church had been influenced by the powerful Greek philosophy which denied the concept of a physical resurrection. The Greeks held a concept of philosophical dualism which is usually attributed to Plato. They believed the physical body was evil and the soul was good. Plato taught that the human body was a prison that encased the soul. At death the soul escaped from the body. The Greeks had a proverb which said, "The body is a tomb and I am a poor soul shackled to a corpse." The idea of a physical resurrection was abhorrent to the Greek mind for it would mean a return to prison.

The confusion in the Corinthian church stemmed from a belief in the bodily resurrection of Christ and a misconception, influenced by Greek thought, about their own resurrection. This led Paul to write, "Now if Christ is preached, that He has been raised from the dead, how do some among you say that there is no resurrection of the dead? But if there is no resurrection of the dead, not even Christ has been raised . . ." (1 Corinthians 15:12, 13).

If they accepted the bodily resurrection of Christ, then they must accept their own physical resurrection. They must either accept the truth of Christ's resurrection or parrot the view of Greek philosophy, but they could not believe both.

## The Physical Resurrection of Christ

The basis of Paul's argument in 1 Corinthians 15 is Christological. He assumes the full incarnation, the fact that Christ was 100 percent God and 100 percent man. The physical attributes of Christ's body are set forth in several New Testament texts:

> Born of a woman (Matthew 1:18)
> Natural birth (Matthew 1:25)
> Circumcised according to law (Luke 2:21)
> Possessed a human soul (Matthew 26:38)
> Possessed a human body (John 1:14)
> Grew in stature and wisdom (Luke 2:52)

Cried (John 11:35)
Experienced hunger (Matthew 4:2)
Experienced thirst (John 19:28)
Was sleepy (Matthew 8:24)
Grew weary (John 4:6)
Felt sorrow, grief, and pain (John 11:38)
Beaten with fists (Luke 22:63)
Beaten with a whip (Matthew 27:26)
Body nailed to a cross (Luke 23:33)
Died physically (John 19:30)
Side pierced with a spear (John 19:34)
Body wrapped and buried (Matthew 27:59)

After the resurrection of Christ, the New Testament reveals the fact that His body still retained physical features:

Could be handled or touched (Luke 24:39)
Walked and talked (Luke 24:13-32)
Broke bread (Luke 24:30)
Ate broiled fish (Luke 24:42, 43)
Breathed air (John 20:22)
Could be recognized (Matthew 28:9,17)
Demonstrated scars of crucifixion (Luke 24:40)

However, the resurrected body of Christ manifested a new state of glory and power:

Appeared and disappeared instantaneously
   (Luke 24:31)
Able to change form or appearance (Mark 16:12)
Could go through walls (John 20:19, 26)
Incorruptible (Acts 1:11 )
Powerful (Acts 1:11 )
Glorified (John 20:5-7)

The concept of Christ's resurrection was different from both the Jewish thought and Greek philosophy. The Jewish rabbis taught that the resurrection body would be exactly like the physical body. The writer of the Apocolypse of Baruch asks about the changes that will take place in the resurrection. The rabbi answered that there will be no change in form, the earth will restore the dead, and the body will remain the same.[4] The Greeks made light of this idea, calling it the "hope of worms." They believed once the soul left the body, it was free forever. Paul presented Christ's resurrection as a physical resurrection that resulted in a glorified transformation of the physical body into a state of immortality. While the physical body of Christ retained its human features, it also demonstrated "superhuman" capabilities.

## Christ's Resurrection and Ours

There are two significant passages which teach that our resurrected bodies will be exactly like Christ's:

> For our citizenship is in heaven, from which also we eagerly wait for a Savior, the Lord Jesus Christ, who will transform the body of our humble state *into conformity with* the body of His glory, by the exertion of the power that He has even to subject all things to Himself (Philippians 3:20, 21; emphasis added).

> Beloved, now we are children of God and it has not appeared as yet what we shall be. We know that, when He appears, *we shall be like Him* because we shall see him just as He is (1 John 3:2; emphasis added).

Since the resurrected body of Jesus retained its physical attributes, in a glorified state, we can assume that the same will be true with us.

Paul wrote, "That which you sow does not come to life unless it dies; and that which you sow, you do not sow the body which is to be, but a bare grain, perhaps of wheat or of something else. But God gives it a body just as He wished, and to each of the seed a body of its own" (1 Corinthians 15:36-38). The resurrected body will be one that is perfectly adapted for fellowship with God. The body that is sown (i.e., the physical body) will take on a more glorified body at the resurrection. Paul continued this thought in verses 42-44, "It is sown a perishable body, it (the physical body, B.R.S.) is raised an imperishable body; it is raised in dishonor, it is raised in glory; it is sown in weakness, it is raised in power; it is sown a natural body, it is raised a spiritual body. If there is a natural body, there is also a spiritual body."

The chief argument the Greeks had against a physical resurrection was the fact that the physical body was corruptible and subject to decay. Note the series of contrasts in the above text:

corruption—incorruption
dishonor—glory
weakness—power

In verse 44 Paul calls the resurrection body a "spiritual body." In the Greek the phrase is "pneumatikon soma" which means a body especially designed for spiritual life. The physical body will be raised and transformed into a substantial body perfectly fitted for a new existence in the spiritual world.

To the Greeks Paul was saying, "In the resurrection you will have a substantial body." To the rabbis Paul said, "When you are raised, you will have a different kind of body, yet it will be related to the seed that was sown—the physical body."

## After His Ascension

Those who reject the idea of a glorified physical body will argue that Christ accommodated Himself to human vision, but after His ascension His body was changed into a spiritual, non-substantial form. Two passages are used to enforce this argument. One is John 20:17, which is the occasion when Jesus appeared to Mary at the tomb following His resurrection. Apparently Mary made some effort to hold on to Jesus. His reply was, "Stop clinging to Me, for I have not yet ascended to the Father, but go to My brethren, and say to them, I ascend to My Father and your Father, and My God and your God." The other passage is 1 Corinthians 15:50, "Now I say this, brethren, that flesh and blood cannot inherit the kingdom of God."

In the case with Mary, she apparently thought that she could once again enjoy Jesus' presence in the same way as before, prior to death. Westcott observed, "She assumed that the return to the old life exhausted the extent of her Master's victory over death."[5] It was important for Mary to realize that her relationship with Christ would be different. His ascension to the Father would mean that Mary's love for the Lord must enter into a new kind of relationship—a relationship based on faith. Because of her great love, Mary was given the opportunity to be the first witness to bear the words of the risen Christ.

The term "flesh and blood" as it is used in 1 Corinthians 15:50 refers to the physical person in a natural state. The same term is used in Hebrews 2:14, "Since then the children share in flesh and blood, He Himself likewise also partook of the same. . . ." The phrase "denotes the whole man in his weak, perishable, corruptible human nature."[6] Paul is simply saying that the natural man cannot enter the kingdom in the physical state—the body must be transformed.

Since His ascension, Christ now dwells in "unapproachable light" (1 Timothy 6:16); nevertheless, the Bible indicates that He still retains the physical form as He had before His ascension. "This Jesus, who has been taken up from you into heaven, will come in *just the same way* as you have watched Him go into heaven" (Acts 1:11; emphasis added). In Revelation 1:10-17 there is recorded a description of Christ in His glorified state, yet with physical characteristics (i.e., hands, hair, feet, eyes, etc.).

The appearance of Christ to Saul of Tarsus on the Damascus Road recorded in Acts 9:1-9 also demonstrated a physical manifestation in a glorified state. Kenneth Boa concluded, "Apparently then, Christ willfully held back His true glory and light while He was in the presence of sinful men on the earth after the resurrection. No mortal eyes would have been able to stand the intensity of His glory if He had not done this. He is still in His resurrection body of glorified flesh as He will forever be."[7]

## The Great Transformation

As we have looked at the antinomy of the resurrection, we've observed the following facts:

1. Our physical body will be raised.
2. The physical body will be transformed into an incorruptible, glorified, and powerful body.
3. The transformed body will be able to serve God in a new spiritual dimension.
4. Death is like the planting of a seed into the ground. It decomposes and springs forth in new life.
5. There will be a continuity between the old physical body and the new glorified body.

Burton Scott Easton wrote,

> The connection of this body (resurrected body, B.R.S.) with the present body is not discussed, except for saying that some connection exists, with the necessity of a transformation for those alive at the end. In this state nothing remains that is inconsistent with the height to which man is raised, and in particular sexual relations (Mark 12:25) and the processes of nutrition (1 Corinthians 6:13) cease. For this end the whole power of God is available. And it is insured by the perfect trust the believer may put in God and by the resurrection of Christ, with Whom the believer has become intimately united. The unrighteous are raised for the final vindication of God's dealings in history.[8]

What great hope the resurrection of Christ gives to the Christian! There are many mysteries that surround the subject of the resurrected body. Our present finite minds are not equipped to deal with nor understand the various aspects of this profound subject. A recent Gallup Poll conducted for twenty-nine religious groups revealed that 68 percent of the unchurched believe in the resurrection of Christ as compared to 93 percent of churchgoers. It is a subject that cannot be treated lightly. Its truth gives profound meaning to life. The Christian's hope centers in the fact that "in Christ all shall be made alive" (1 Corinthians 15:22).

The implications of the resurrection of Jesus Christ from the dead are enormous:

1. It means that Jesus was who He claimed to be—the Son of God.
2. It means that Jesus is the only way to God.
3. It means that through the cross, there is forgiveness available and the possibility of a new beginning.
4. It means there is life after death.
5. It means there is hope for this world.
6. It means out of suffering can come new power and a better life.
7. It means God will one day judge the world in righteousness (Acts 17:31).

Christianity is the only religion of the world that exists on the basis of the death and resurrection of its leader. All other world religions exist on the basis of the teaching that the leaders gave. Christianity would not exist one day, in spite of its good moral principles, apart from the belief that Christ is alive. Everything pertaining to Christ rests on this one statement: "He was raised on the third day according to the Scriptures" (1 Corinthians 15:4).

## Notes

[1]John MacArthur Jr., *Resurrection Truth*, (Panorama City, CA: Word of Grace Communications, 1981), p. 11.

[2]C. F. Evans, *Resurrection and the New Testament*, (Naperville: Allenson, 1920), p. 1.

[3]J. N. D. Anderson, *Christianity The Witness of History* (Downers Grove, IL: Inter Varsity Press, 1970), p. 13.

[4]John MacArthur Jr., p. 62.

[5]B. F. Westcott, *The Gospel According to St. John* (Grand Rapids, MI: Wm. B. Eerdmans Publishing Co., 1962), p. 292.

[6]J. A. Schep, *The Nature of the Resurrection Body* (Grand Rapids, MI: Wm. B. Eerdmans Publishing Co., 1964), p. 203.

[7]Kenneth Boa, *God, I Don't Understand* (Wheaton, IL: Victor Books, 1975), pp. 79-80.

[8]Burton Scott Easton, "Resurrection" in *The International Standard Bible Encyclopedia*, Vol. IV (Grand Rapids, MI: Wm. B. Eerdmans Publishing Co., 1939), pp. 2564-2565.

## Remembering the Facts

1. What is the antinomy in the biblical doctrine of the resurrection?

2. How many times is the resurrection mentioned in the New Testament?

3. How does Job 19:25-27 prove that Job believed in a bodily resurrection?

4. What influence did Greek philosophy have on the early church? How did that philosophy clash with the teaching concerning Christ's resurrection?

5. What evidence in the New Testament supports the physical resurrection of Christ's body? What evidence supports its transformation into a glorified state?

6. How will our physical bodies be like Christ's body in the resurrection?

7. In 1 Corinthians 15:14, Paul refers to the resurrected body as a "spiritual body." What is the meaning of this term?

8. What does the term "flesh and blood" refer to?

9. What scriptural evidence is there to prove that Christ's resurrected body did not change after the ascension?

10. List the five things which the New Testament reveals concerning the resurrected body:

   (1)


   (2)


   (3)


   (4)


   (5)


## Discussing the Issues

1. What significance does the resurrection of Christ have on our daily trials and difficulties or on the way we live our lives?

2. The Scriptures teach that at the resurrection, our physical bodies will be brought to life in a glorified state. Discuss the implications of that doctrine in connection with the following:

   cremation vs. burial

infant death

recognition of one another in heaven

3. Since both the righteous and unrighteous shall be raised, what do you believe will happen to the physical body of the unrighteous person?

4. Do you believe enough emphasis is placed on the resurrection of Christ in the church today? Discuss the implications of neglect.

# Chapter 12
# God's Presence—Near or Far?

> For Thou art the Lord Most High over all the earth;
> ... our God is in the heavens; ... (Psalm 97:9;
> 115:3).
>
> He is not far from each one of us; for in Him we live
> and move and exist... (Acts 17:27, 28).

Almost every child that has been taught about God has wondered at one time or another, "Where does God live?" The common answer that most parents give is that God is in heaven. While this is correct to a point, it fails to convey the whole truth. The problem is we cannot point to a place and say, "There is God's dwelling place."

In the Old Testament God's presence (the Shekinah) was in the temple. "And it came about when the priests came from the holy place, that the cloud filled the house of the Lord, so that the priests could not stand to minister because of the cloud, for the glory of the Lord filled the house of the Lord" (1 Kings 8:10, 11). However, Solomon realized that the temple could not contain God. He said, "But will God indeed dwell on the earth? Behold, heaven and the highest heaven cannot contain Thee, how much less this house which I have built!" (1 Kings 8:27).

The Bible reveals that God is outside space and time and yet He is very much a part of His creation. In this chapter we will conduct a fascinating study on the antinomy of God's transcendental and personal nature.

## Omnipresence

The term "omnipresence" is not found in the Bible. However, it is a word that graphically describes a characteristic of God revealed in the Bible. Omnipresence means that God is everywhere present at once. The *whole* of God is in every place at the same time. " 'Am I a God who is near,' declares the Lord, 'and not a God far off? Can a man hide himself in hiding places so I do not see him?' declares the Lord. 'Do I not fill the heavens and the earth?' declares the Lord" (Jeremiah 23:23, 24). God is speaking through the prophet Jeremiah and revealing Himself as capable of being near and far as well as being able to see every hiding place that man may occupy. He even goes a step further and declares that He is present *everywhere* in the heavens and the earth.

Psalm 139 is perhaps one of the most fascinating chapters in the Bible. It reveals three aspects of God's character. It may be divided into the following parts:

### God's Omniscience

O Lord, Thou hast searched me and known me,
Thou dost know when I sit down and when I rise up;
Thou dost understand my thought from afar.
Thou dost scrutinize my path and my lying down,
And art intimately acquainted with all my ways.
Even before there is a word on my tongue,
Behold, O Lord, Thou dost know it all.
Thou hast enclosed me behind and before,
And laid Thy hand upon me.
Such knowledge is too wonderful for me;
It is too high, I cannot attain it.

### God's Omnipresence

Where can I go from Thy Spirit?
Or where can I flee from Thy presence?
If I ascend to heaven, Thou art there;
If I make my bed in Sheol, behold, Thou art there.
If I take the wings of the dawn,

If I dwell in the remotest part of the sea,
Even there Thy hand will lead me,
And Thy right hand will lay hold of me.
If I say, "Surely the darkness will overwhelm me,
And the light around me will be night,"
Even the darkness is not dark to Thee,
And the night is as bright as the day.
Darkness and light are alike to Thee.

### God's Omnipotence

For Thou didst form my inward parts;
Thou didst weave me in my mother's womb.
I will give thanks to Thee, for I am fearfully and
   wonderfully made;
Wonderful are Thy works,
And my soul knows it very well.
My frame was not hidden from Thee
When I was made in secret
And skillfully wrought in the depths of the earth.
Thine eyes have seen my unformed substance;
And in Thy book they were all written
The days that were ordained for me,
When as yet there was not one of them.
How precious also are Thy thoughts to me, O God!
How vast is the sum of them!
If I should count them, they would outnumber the sand.
When I awake, I am still with Thee.

Some people find it hard to believe that God is always present since they cannot see, feel, hear, or know that He is there. When a Russian astronaut returned from outer space, he declared that he did not see God anywhere. Of course, no one expected that he would since the Bible reveals that God is invisible. "He who is the blessed and only Sovereign, the King of kings and Lord of lords; who alone possesses immortality and dwells in unapproachable light; *whom no man has seen or can see*. To Him be honor and eternal dominion!" (1 Timothy 6:15, 16; emphasis added).

Perhaps a good illustration to help us appreciate God's omnipresence is radio and television waves. All around us there are pictures and sounds which we cannot hear, feel, or see. These pictures and sounds are being broadcast over radio waves. The only way to pick up these waves is by using a proper receiver (television or radio). However, the fact that we are unable to see these pictures with the naked eye or hear the sounds with our unaided ears does not make these TV waves nonexistent. With or without our capacity to receive these messages, they still exist.

## Omnipresence Is Not Pantheism

Some ancients were pantheists. They believed that there were gods in every place. According to their belief, gods inhabited individual trees, stones, and even idols fashioned by the hands of men. The psalmist declared that God is not in any one place alone:

Why should the nations say,
Where, now, is their God?
But our God is in the heavens;
He does whatever He pleases.
Their idols are silver and gold,
The work of man's hands.
They have mouths, but they cannot speak;
They have eyes, but they cannot see;
They have ears, but they cannot hear;
They have noses, but they cannot smell;
They have hands, but they cannot feel;
They have feet, but they cannot walk.
They cannot make a sound with their throat.
Those who make them will become like them,
Everyone who trusts in them (Psalm 115:2-8).

Pantheism perverts omnipresence to mean that nature, which is sustained and upheld by God, becomes God, too. Pantheism confuses the created with the Creator. It substitutes the complex for the simple and thus perverts this marvelous concept of God. Trees and mountains are not God. God does not take on the form of nature in any way, even though He is present in trees, mountains, and animals. All of nature reveals the majesty and grandeur of God. But nature can never contain God.

Augustine summed up the omnipresence of God in one of his marvelous essays:

> You fill the heaven and the earth. Do they therefore contain You? . . . When heaven and earth are filled with You, into what do You pour that surplus of Yourself which remains over? Or is it not rather the case that You have no need to be contained by anything? . . . You who fill everything are wholly present in everything which You fill. Or can we say that, because all things together are unable to contain You wholly, therefore each thing contains only a part of You? Does every thing contain the same part? Or are there different parts for different things in accordance with the varying sizes of the things? That would mean that some parts of You could be greater and some smaller than others. Shall we not rather say this: everywhere You are present in Your entirety, and no single thing can contain You in Your entirety?[1]

## Transcendent and Immanent

The correct view of God, therefore, is that He is both transcendent and immanent (remaining near or within). To say that God is transcendent means that He is exalted above and is distinct from the created order, the universe. "To Thee I lift up my eyes, O Thou who art enthroned in the heavens!" (Psalm 123:1). "The Lord is high above all nations; His glory is above the heavens. Who is like the Lord our God, who is enthroned on high?" (Psalm 113:4, 5).

The immanence of God means He pervades and sustains all creation. "He is before all things and in Him all things hold together" (Colossians 1:17). Speaking of Jesus the Hebrew writer declared, "He is the radiance of His glory and the exact representation of His nature, and upholds all things by the word of His power" (Hebrews 1:3).

Again, it is difficult for people to think of God in terms of this antinomy. For example, about the time of the French revolution a number of theologians began to take the position that God had created the world but then had withdrawn from it and was no longer involved with or related to its ongoing order. These were called deists. While today deism is dead in so far as an organized religion is concerned, nevertheless, many people are still deists. They do not perceive God as an active force in the world today. The Bible reveals that God is both beyond this world and at the same time integrally intertwined in it at every place and time.

Francis Schaeffer, in his marvelous book *He Is There and He Is Not Silent*, reveals a tremendous insight into God's personal presence and infinite nature.

> Let us return again to the personal-infinite. On the side of God's infinity, there is a complete chasm between God on one side and man, the animal, the flower, and the machine on the other. On the side of God's infinity, he stands alone. He is the absolute other. He is, in his infinity, contrary to all else. He is differentiated from all else because only he is infinite. He is the Creator; all else was created. He is infinite; all else is finite. All else is brought forth by creation, so all else is dependent and only he is independent. This is absolute on the side of his infinity. Therefore, concerning God's infinity, man is as separated from God as is the atom or any other machine-portion of the universe.
>
> But on the side of God being personal, the chasm is between man and the animal, the plant, and the machine. Why? Because man was made in the image of God. This is not just "doctrine." It is dogma that needs just to be repeated linearly, as McLuhan would say. This is really down in the warp and woof of the whole problem. Man is made in the image of God; therefore, on the side of the fact that God is a personal God the chasm stands not between God and

man, but between man and all else. But on the side of God's infinity, man is as separated from God as the atom or any other finite of the universe. So we have the answer to man's being finite and yet personal.

It is not that this is the best answer to existence; it is the only answer. That is why we may hold our Christianity with intellectual integrity. The only answer for what exists is that he, the infinite-personal God, really is there.[2]

## The "I-Thou" Relationship

The term "I-Thou" was created by Martin Buber, a Jewish philosopher. He used this term to describe personal relationships in which the other person is always treated as a person, not a thing. The "I-Thou" relationship avoids manipulation and abuse of others. Its goal is respectability and honor, recognizing the personal worth that every person has. It suggests a very personal, intimate relationship with another human being. For this reason, it is a good term to use in reference to our relationship with God.

When we speak of a personal relationship with God, we assume that the common sense distinction between God and things is accurate. We affirm that God is more like a person than a thing. He is more like a father than an abstract object.

God revealed Himself throughout the Bible as a loving, personal Father. "And the Lord said to Moses, 'When you go back to Egypt . . . then you shall say to Pharaoh, "Thus says the Lord. 'Israel is My son, My firstborn. So I said to you, "Let My son go, that he may serve Me"; but you refused to let him go. Behold, I will kill your son, your firstborn' " ' " (Exodus 4:21-23). When God chose Israel in its youth, Hosea revealed God's relationship as one of a father: "When Israel was a youth I loved him, and out of Egypt I called My son" (Hosea 11:1).

God revealed His Fatherhood to David's son Solomon. Speaking through inspiration, David said, "And He said to me, 'Your son Solomon is the one who shall build My house and My courts;

for I have chosen him to be a son to Me, and I will be a Father to him' " (1 Chronicles 28:6). God's great prophets continued to reveal the personal Fatherhood of God. "Listen, O heavens, and hear, O earth; for the Lord speaks, 'Sons I have reared and brought up, but they have revolted against Me. An ox knows its owner, and a donkey its master's manger, but Israel does not know, My people do not understand' " (Isaiah 1: 2, 3). "Then I said, 'How I would set you among My sons, and give you a pleasant land, the most beautiful inheritance of the nations!' And I said, 'You shall call Me, My Father, and not turn away from following Me' " (Jeremiah 3:19).

Jesus continued this revelation of the Father-child relationship during His ministry on earth. On one occasion He said, "See that you do not despise one of these little ones for I say to you, that their angels in heaven continually behold the face of My Father who is in heaven . . . Thus it is not the will of your Father who is in heaven that one of these little ones perish" (Matthew 18:10, 14). When Jesus taught His disciples to pray, He began with the words, "Our Father who art in heaven . . ." (Matthew 6:9).

Jesus also introduced a new dimension to God's progressive revelation of His personal relationship with His creatures. Jesus chose the Aramaic word "Abba" to refer to God as our Father. This word is different from the Hebrew word for father (Ab) and the Greek word for father (Paterno). The Aramaic language was spoken by the Jews in New Testament times. It was a language related to Hebrew in some respects. The word Abba is similar to our English words dad and daddy. There are three passages in the New Testament where this word is used to refer to God— Mark 14:32-37; Romans 8:14-17; Galatians 4:4-7. The word Abba suggests a very close, personal, intimate relationship with God. To be able to call God Abba means we are aware of His intimate relationship with us on a very personal basis.

It is important to realize that God's omnipresence does not mean some kind of mystical abstraction. God is a personal being with mind, emotion, and will. He has knowledge and feelings. He is a divine being and a supreme personality, but these qualities must not stand beyond His personality. God is not something; He is somebody. He is not only present everywhere, He is also intimately involved and personally acquainted with every person on earth.

## God's Indwelling

The most amazing part of God's presence is the reality of His personal indwelling in the individual believer. "Jesus answered and said to him, 'If anyone loves Me, he will keep My word; and My Father will love him, and We will come to him and make Our abode with him' " (John 14:23). Paul declared that there is "One God and Father of all who is over all and through all and in all" (Ephesians 4:6).

Jesus also taught that He would dwell personally within every believer. "In that day you shall know that I am in My Father and you in Me, and I in you" (John 14:20). Paul wrote, "I have been crucified with Christ; and it is no longer I who lives, but Christ lives in Me" (Galatians 2:20). The Bible also speaks of "Christ in you, the hope of glory" (Colossians 1:27).

The third member of the Trinity also dwells in the Christian. "However you are not in the flesh but in the Spirit, if indeed the Spirit of Christ dwells in you. But if anyone does not have the Spirit of Christ, he does not belong to Him" (Romans 8:9). "Or do you not know that your body is a temple of the Holy Spirit who is in you, whom you have from God, and that you are not your own?" (1 Corinthians 6:19).

Even though God is omnipresent, filling the heavens and earth, yet He does not dwell in all things in a personal way. God does not dwell among unbelieving, unregenerate people (c.f., Hosea 1:6).

John R. W. Stott has explained well the gulf that exists between a holy God and sinful man:

> If the curtain which veils the unspeakable majesty of God could be drawn aside but for a moment, we too should not be able to bear the sight. As it is, we only dimly perceive how pure and brilliant must be the glory of almighty God. However, we know enough to

realize that sinful man while still in his sins can never approach this holy God. A great chasm yawns between God in his righteousness and man in his sin.[3]

God's personal indwelling is selective, limited only to those who respond in trusting faith to Jesus Christ. Thus God is able to limit His presence in some way and in different degrees (c.f., 1 Kings 19:11 f).

## The Revelation of His Names

One of the marvelous aspects of God's personal nature is the progressive revelation of His presence and power in the names of God which are found in Scripture. Here is a list for your personal study and reflection:

| | | |
|---|---|---|
| Genesis 22:14 | Jehovah-Jireh | "I am the One who provides" |
| Exodus 15:26 | Jehovah-Rapha | "I am the One who heals" |
| Exodus 17:15 | Jehovah-Nissi" | "I am thy banner" |
| Judges 6:24 | Jehovah-Shalom | "I am thy peace" |
| Psalm 23:1 | Jehovah-Ra-ah | "I am thy Shepherd" |
| Jeremiah 23:6 | Jehovah-Tsidkenu | "I am thy righteousness" |
| Ezekiel 48:35 | Jehovah-Shammah | "I am the One who is there" |

## Avoiding Extremes

As is true with all antinomies of Scripture, we must avoid the extremes. God cannot be reduced to human terms and descriptions. While it is true that God is like us, it is also true that He transcends persons as we understand them. To transcend is to be higher and greater. To affirm that God is personal is not to say He has a body like us or that He thinks and acts as we do. It is important to keep the balance!

Twentieth-century theologians have demonstrated both extremes. One group called the personalists believes that God is personal but not absolute. This is a rather attractive position for those who have difficulty with the problem of evil. The personalists say that God is not *all*-powerful. If He were, evil would be destroyed. But according to this view there are limits to what God can do. A good example of this theology is found in Rabbi Kushner's best-selling book *When Bad Things Happen to Good People*. Kushner believes that man "is only the latest stage in a long, slow evolutionary process."[4] He sees the tragedies of life as a part of that process. God is simply not big enough to do something about the "bad things" that happen to people.

The other extreme affirms that God is absolute and not personal. Some modern examples of this extreme are seen in the writings of Barth, Brunner, and Tillich. Paul Tillich described the non-personal aspect of God in the following way:

> The God who is a being is transcended by the God who is Being itself, the ground and abyss of every being. And the God who is a person is transcended by the God who is the Personal-Itself, the ground and abyss of every person.[5]

Maintaining the balance between extremes will result in a greater faith in God's power and a greater awareness of His personal presence in our lives. Our fear of God's awesome presence can be balanced with reverence and comfort because of His loving care and protection of our lives. This inspires greater obedience from us as we live under the watchful eye of His ever-present Majesty. His presence is with us no matter where we go or what happens to us.

> The story is told of a weary Christian who had a dream. In this dream he saw two sets of footprints walking along the sand. Suddenly he noticed that several yards back one set disappeared and only one set continued. When this Christian met the Lord in heaven he complained that Christ had been untrue to His promise to walk with him all the way and had obviously, somehow, forsaken him in his need.

"No," replied the Lord. "Where the two sets of prints become one is the point at which you walked through deep valleys. The reason there was only one set of footprints from that point forward is because then I began carrying you."[6]

There are so many mysteries surrounding God and His relationship with us, but some day all those mysteries will be cleared up when we see Him face to face. I have an idea that we will receive many wonderful surprises about His love and care in our lives, just as the above story illustrates. But for now, we have the privilege of growing, learning, and worshiping the One in whom we live, move, and exist.

## Notes

[1]*The Confessions of St. Augustine*, translated by Rex Warner (New York: The New American Library, 1963), pp. 18-19.

[2]Francis Schaeffer, *He Is There and He Is Not Silent* (Wheaton, IL: Tyndale House Publishers, 1972), pp. 14-15.

[3]John R. W. Stott, *Basic Christianity* (Downers Grove, IL: Inter Varsity Press, 1958), p. 73.

[4]Harold S. Kushner, *When Bad Things Happen to Good People* (New York: Schocken, 1981), p. 65.

[5]Paul Tillich, as quoted by Fisher Humphreys, *Thinking About God* (New Orleans: Insight Press, 1974), p. 63.

[6]John Bisagno, *God Is* (Wheaton, IL: Victor Books, 1983), p. 98.

## Remembering the Facts

1. What is the meaning of the term "omnipresence"? Give some Scripture to support this doctrine.

2. Why do some people find this a difficult doctrine to accept?

3. How is the doctrine of omnipresence different from pantheism?

4. Define these terms:
   Transcendent—

   Immanent—

5. What position did the deists take relative to God's presence?

6. What is the meaning of the "I-Thou" relationship as it pertains to man and God?

7. What new dimension did Jesus introduce concerning God's personal relationship with His creatures?

8. Give some Scriptures that support the Godhead's personal indwelling in the believer:
   God the Father—

   God the Son—

   God the Holy Spirit—

9. List the seven names of God in the Old Testament. Write the definition of each one.
   (1)

(2)

(3)

(4)

(5)

(6)

(7)

10. What blessings may we expect as a result of maintaining a proper balance between God's personal presence and His transcendental nature?

## Discussing the Issues

1. Why is it difficult to believe that God is involved with or related to the ongoing order of this world?

2. One of the personal, human aspects attributed to God is repentance. Discuss how God repents.

3. What are some of the dangers involved in attributing human characteristics to God?

4. How should the transcendent nature of God affect our worship?

## Chapter 13
# Faith—Rational or Subjective?

If our heart does not condemn us, we have confidence before God; . . . (1 John 3:21).

. . . for the Lord will be your confidence, . . . (Proverbs 3:26).

In what does the Christian find confidence—the heart? Or the Lord? To ask it another way, is Christian faith subjective or objective? Does the Christian believe God because it "feels good" to believe, or is faith a result of rational, logical deduction? The Bible seems to answer "yes" to both questions.

There are places in Scripture that seem to indicate that faith is produced subjectively. "If any man is willing to do His will, he shall know of the teaching, whether it is of God, or whether I speak from myself" (John 7:17). This verse implies that faithful obedience to God's commands will verify by experience the validity of Christ's teaching. B. F. Westcott commented on this verse, "The force of the argument lies in the moral harmony of the man's purpose with the divine law so far as this law is known or felt. If there be no sympathy there can be no understanding. Religion is a matter of life and not of thought only."[1] The conclusion, therefore, is that faith is produced through subjective experimentation with God's law. The more one obeys the law of God, the more convinced one becomes that this is the best way to live, and faith is in turn strengthened through that experience.

Paul wrote, "Do not be conformed to this world, but be transformed by the renewing of your mind, that you may prove what the will of God is, that which is good and acceptable and perfect" (Romans 12:2). The word "prove" means to "try and approve" the will of God. The fact is that God's will is always good, acceptable, and perfect, but Paul is saying that the Christian needs to discover in his/her own life experience that God's will is equivalent to the good, acceptable, and perfect. The conclusion is that faith cannot possibly be a matter of rational deduction alone. There is a sense in which faith cannot exist without the subjective, the "heart experience." Paul wrote, "You became obedient from the heart to that form of teaching . . ." (Romans 6:17).

So here is the antinomy—faith must be a matter of logical reasoning and deduction. "For every house is built by someone, but the builder of all things is God" (Hebrews 3:4). This is a logical deduction—just as a house demonstrates the fact that a designer and constructor built it, just so the world we live in demonstrates the fact that a Designer and Creator exists. "By faith we understand that the worlds were prepared by the word of God . . ." (Hebrews 11:3). Faith in God as Creator is a matter of logical deduction. Yet we have observed from Scripture that faith is also an outgrowth of experimenting with God's will to verify its truthfulness in our lives.

Perhaps this antinomy answers the question as to why the non-Christian finds it so hard to have faith, even after many "air-tight" arguments have been presented in favor of God and Christianity. Until a person is willing to make a commitment of life to God, a strong faith in God will never be produced. In the words of Kierkegaard, one must make a "leap of faith" into the unknown. Only then will the truth of God be discovered insofar as each individual is concerned.

There is a point in everyone's conversion experience at which the person must cry out with the father of the demon-possessed boy, "I do believe, help me in my unbelief" (Mark 9:24). At that point, the "leap of faith" must be taken. When one reaches a place of total despair with nowhere to turn but to God, perhaps more than any other, this is the time faith develops muscle and becomes real and vibrant. At this point God's Spirit leads one to cast one's self totally upon Christ. At that moment, faith becomes reality.

## The Sin Problem

The greatest difficulty which man has in coming to God in faith is the sin problem. Sin prevents man from allowing the Creator to be God. The first human sin was a yielding to the temptation to be like God (Genesis 3:5). J. I. Packer made this penetrating observation about sin, "Sin is exalting oneself against the Creator, withholding the homage due to Him, and putting oneself in His place as the ultimate standard of reference in life's decisions."[2] Dr. Packer then quoted Augustine who analyzed sin as pride (superbia), the mad passion to be superior even to God, and as a state of being bent away from God into an attitude of self-absorption (homo incurvatus inse).

Sin is the devil's control over human life with self-exalting pride preventing the person from realizing a need for God's presence or control in life. In this condition, man finds it impossible to have a strong faith in God. "A natural man does not accept the things of the Spirit of God; for they are foolishness to him, and he cannot understand them, because they are spiritually appraised" (1 Corinthians 2:14).

It must be understood at this point that the truth of Christianity is not existential or subjective. Christianity is true whether or not anyone ever verifies its truthfulness. J. Gresham Machen wrote,

> That does not mean that Christianity is true only for those who thus will to accept it, and that it is not true for others; on the contrary it is true, we think, even for the demons in hell as well as the saints in heaven, though its truth does the demons no good. But for a thing to be true is one thing and for it to be recognized as true is another; and in order that Christianity may be recognized as true by men upon this earth the blinding effects of sin must be removed. The blinding effects of sin are removed by the Spirit of God; and the Spirit chooses to do that only for those whom He brings by the new birth into the kingdom of God. Regeneration, or the new birth, therefore, does not stand in opposition to a truly scientific

attitude toward the evidence, but on the contrary it is necessary in order that the truly scientific attitude may be attained; it is not a substitute for the intellect, but on the contrary by it the intellect is made to be a trustworthy instrument for apprehending the truth.[3]

The truth of the gospel cannot be established intellectually until the "blinding effects of sin" are removed. That can only happen when a person steps out by faith and responds to the gospel of Christ. In that response, the validity of the gospel through God's Spirit becomes a reality in the Christian's life. Faith is verified and thus becomes viable and vital. So faith begins in the intellect, but will never grow until the will makes a commitment to God. That commitment will in turn strengthen and enlarge faith as the will of God is proven to be good and acceptable and perfect. Intellectual or rational faith must give rise to subjective faith which then gives validity to the intellectual. But first the barrier of sin must be removed in order for real faith to grow.

## The Movement of Repentance

Martin Luther once received a letter from a close friend that said, "I have promised God a thousand times that I would become a better man, but I never kept my promise. I am not going to make any more vows. Experience has taught me that I cannot keep them. Unless God is merciful to me for Christ's sake, and grants me a new departure, I shall not be able to stand before him." Luther's comment was that this is "God-pleasing despair."[4]

A good definition of repentance is "God-pleasing despair." God desires that we be honest about ourselves before Him. When we are, we experience despair. We must acknowledge that we have nothing to offer Him but our sin and failures.

When Jesus came announcing the "kingdom of God is at hand," His next words were, "repent and believe in the gospel"

(Mark 1:15). You will note that repentance precedes faith in the gospel. This same order is found in Acts 20:21 where Paul spoke of "repentance toward God and faith in our Lord Jesus Christ." Repentance must precede genuine faith because repentance means the individual has ceased "play-acting" and is throwing himself on the mercy of God. It is a movement away from self and self-regarding motives as well as rebellion and a movement toward God, relying wholly upon His forgiveness and love. Only then can faith become reality in one's experience.

Robert Johnson writes penetratingly,

> We should notice that this movement of repentance is made possible by the cross. Apart from a sense of what Christ did in giving His life for us, we cannot repent. When we can see no way out, we will not accept the fact that we are what we are. Nor can we confess the truth about ourselves to God. Rather, we pull our cloak of hypocrisy and pretense closer about us and "play-act"—in the futile, frustrating attempt to convince ourselves, others, and God that we really are not what we are (or, at least, will not be for long).
>
> It is the "good news" that God has given us through the cross that permits us to be ourselves *before* Him, and to present our unvarnished selves to Him. When we see that Christ has "taken our place" and that through Christ's sacrifice of His life God is holding out to us unconditional forgiveness and love, we can turn and accept this forgiveness and love *in spite* of our complete unworthiness of it. To do so is to repent.[5]

Once that repentance has become real, faith or trust in Jesus Christ becomes absolutely necessary. As a matter of fact, there is no alternative. Once a person repents (in the *true* sense of the word), there is nowhere to go but to Jesus Christ. Faith in Christ is an outgrowth of repentance.

The greatest need of every human being is to be able to see what sin is in relation to a holy and righteous God. "Thine eyes are too pure to approve evil, and Thou canst not look on wickedness with favor" (Habakkuk 1:13). The movement of repentance allows the individual to be honest before God about sin. Humility replaces pride (Acts 2:37, 38).

## Balancing the Antinomy

Intellectual faith accepts the truth of God's revelation of Himself to man through the Bible, and subjective faith springs out of the despair of repentance when there is nowhere to go but to Christ. It takes both types of faith to realize salvation. Overemphasis on the intellectual or rational will reduce the Bible and salvation to formulas. One's relationship with God will depend on how much knowledge is possessed. The Bible will become a rule book with very little relevancy to everyday life.

Subjective faith without the rational will lead one into emotionalism, and truth will become a matter of one's own feelings. Spirituality will be measured by the emotional. God will be viewed as a "cosmic genie" who promises health and wealth.

Again, the balance is very important. It is vitally important to possess both rational and subjective faith. Without both, the entire Christian experience will be lopsided.

## Not Middle of the Road

In this book I have shown why it is important to accept both sides of the antinomy which these divine mysteries present. It is important to realize that this is not a "middle-of-the-road" position. Rather, it requires a great deal of faith in God's revelation of Himself in the Bible. The weaker one's faith, the greater will be the tendency to go off into an extreme by maximizing one part of the antinomy and minimizing (or completely abandoning) another part. My purpose in this writing has been to seek for a balanced faith with regard to God's revelation.

There are two results that I can see from this quest for balanced faith:

1. A rich experience of joy and excitement that can only be known by those who accept God's complete revelation of Himself.
2. A unity of believers as people of different faiths (or antinomial beliefs) begin to realize how important a balanced faith really is.

## Christians Only

Religious division is abhorrent to those who have the mind of Christ. Careful examination of the 20,781 organized churches and denominations (see chapter 1) will reveal that the source of most divisions is doctrinal. For centuries theologians have searched for a way to maintain doctrinal unity, but with very little success. Various unity or ecumenical movements have begun only to end up in their own doctrinal debates and divisions. These divisions have come about, in many cases, as a result of an unbalanced approach to scripture. People have gone into extremes with regard to the antinomies of Scripture.

The problem has not been a lack of respect for God's Word, but rather a failure to see the mysteries and complexity of God. God does not ask us to understand the impossible or be able to explain the mysterious; He only asks that we believe Him and take Him at His word. Such is the plea that I am setting forth in this volume. It is a plea for a faith that rests in the grace of Christ alone while allowing for tension to exist in the mysteries of God's revelation.

Charles Simeon, a minister in Cambridge, England for over fifty years, once wrote about his high regard for God's word. I came across Simeon's statement as I was finishing this chapter; however, I do not have the original source for further reference. Simeon wrote:

> I love the simplicity of the scriptures; and I wish
> to receive and communicate every truth precisely in

the way, and to the extent, that it is set forth in the inspired volume.

My endeavor is to bring out of scripture what is there, and not to thrust in what I think might be there. I have a great conviction on this point: never to speak more or less than what I believe to be the mind of the Spirit in the passage I am expounding. I will do nothing else.

It is an invariable rule with me to endeavor to give to every portion of the word of God its full and proper force. Where the inspired writers speak in unqualified terms, I think myself at liberty to do the same, judging that they need no instruction from me as to how to propagate the truth.

I am content to sit as a learner at the feet of the holy apostles, and have no ambition to teach them how they ought to have spoken.

The Bible declares, "The eyes of the Lord move to and fro throughout the earth that He may strongly support those whose heart is completely His" (2 Chronicles 16:9). Such commitment should be the goal of each person's faith—a heart fully committed to the Lord.

Now faith is the assurance of things hoped for, the conviction of things not seen. . . . And without faith it is impossible to please Him, for he who comes to God must believe that He is, and that He is a rewarder of those who seek Him (Hebrews 11:1, 6).

Your faith should not rest on the wisdom of men, but on the power of God (1 Corinthians 2:5).

In addition to all, taking up the shield of faith with which you will be able to extinguish all the flaming missiles of the evil one (Ephesians 6:16).

When you received from us the word of God's message, you accepted it not as the word of men, but for what it really is, the word of God, which also performs its work in you who believe (1 Thessalonians 2:13).

## Notes

[1]B. F. Westcott, *The Gospel According to St. John* (Grand Rapids, MI: Wm. B. Eerdmans Publishing Co., 1962), p. 118.

[2]J. I. Packer, *God's Words* (Downers Grove, IL: Inter Varsity Press, 1981), p. 73.

[3]J. Gresham Machen, *What Is Faith?* (Grand Rapids, MI: Wm. B. Eerdmans Publishing Co., 1946), p. 135.

[4]Robert Clyde Johnson, *The Meaning of Christ* (Philadelphia: The Westminster Press, 1977), p. 91.

[5]Ibid., pp. 91-92.

## Remembering the Facts

1. How is faith produced through subjective experimentation with God's law?

2. How is faith produced by logical reasoning and deduction?

3. What is the greatest difficulty man has in coming to God in faith?

4. What is a good definition of sin?

5. How are the "blinding effects of sin" removed?

6. What is a good definition of repentance?

7. Overemphasis on rational faith or subjective faith can be very dangerous. Explain why.

8. What are the two primary blessings that will come about as a result of a balanced faith?

9. What is one way to avoid the religious division so prevalent today?

## Discussing the Issues

1. Since the Scriptures teach that the more we obey, the greater our faith becomes, how can a Christian develop obedient faith without becoming legalistic in his attitude toward God's law?

2. Discuss the importance of baptism as it relates to subjective faith (i.e., the will making a commitment to God).

3. What effect may continued disobedience have on intellectual faith?

4. How may a Christian lead a loved one or friend to repentance (God-pleasing despair) in order that trust in Christ will result?

# Epilogue

Great is our Lord, and abundant in strength; His understanding is infinite (Psalm 147:5).

No greater pleasure can come to the human mind than that of knowing more about the God who made us and in whose image we were created. This book has explored some of the great mysteries in God's revelation. The journey has been difficult at times, but never boring. You've no doubt found it necessary to rethink some previously held concepts. That's good. We should never reach a place in our search for understanding where we claim to possess all there is to know about a certain subject. Such a conclusion will almost guarantee a limited knowledge of any biblical subject, because God's truth is always greater than the finite mind can conceive or comprehend.

The fallacy of unbelief is seen in the fact that a person can conclude that the human mind is capable of understanding and explaining away the reality of God's presence and activity. A good illustration of this is Mark Twain. He wrote:

A God who could make good children as easily as bad, yet preferred to make bad ones; who could have made every one of them happy, yet never made a single happy one; who made them prize their bitter life, yet stingily cut it short; who gave his angels eternal happiness unearned, yet required his other children to earn it; who gave his angels painless lives, yet cursed his other children with biting miseries and maladies of mind and body; who mouths justice and invented Hell—mouths Golden Rules, and forgiveness multiplied seventy times seven, and invented Hell; who mouths morals to other people and has none himself; who frowns upon crimes, yet commits them all; who created man without invitation, then tries to shuffle the responsibility for man's acts upon man, instead of honorably placing it where it belongs, upon himself; and finally, with altogether divine obtuseness, invites this poor, abused slave to worship him (Mark Twain: The Mysterious Stranger).

Twain's concept of God lacks the balance that good biblical study and responsible research can produce. Unfortunately many Bible students also lack the proper balance as well because the antinomies of Scripture have not been kept in proper perspective.

Once a student develops an antinomial approach to the Word of God, many of the mysteries will become less difficult to accept. Someday we shall be able to see these antinomies in clear light and the mysteries will disappear. "For now we see in a mirror dimly, but then face to face; now I know in part, but then I shall know fully . . ." (1 Corinthians 13:12). Between now and then, we have the glorious privilege of growing and learning more and more about the great God whom we love and serve.

What, then, is my God? I ask, except the Lord God? For who is Lord but the Lord? Or who is God save our God? O highest and best, most powerful, most all-powerful, most merciful and most just, most deeply hidden and most nearly present, most beautiful and most strong, constant yet incomprehensible, changeless, yet changing all things, never new, never old, making all things new; bringing the proud to decay and they know it not; always acting and always at rest; still gathering yet never wanting; upholding, filling and protecting, creating, nourishing and bringing to perfection; seeking, although in need of nothing. You love, but with no storm of passion; You are jealous, but with no anxious fear; You repent, but do not grieve; in Your anger calm; You change Your works, but never change Your plan; You take back what You find and yet have never lost; never in need, You are yet glad of gain; never greedy, yet still demanding profit on Your loans; to be paid in excess, so that You may be the debtor, and yet who has anything which is not Yours? You pay back debts which You never owed and cancel debts without losing anything. And in all this what have I said, my God, my Life, my holy sweetness? What does any man succeed in saying when he attempts to speak of You? Yet woe to those who do not speak of You at all, when those who speak most say nothing (*The Confessions of St. Augustine*, 1:4).

Selected books for further study:

1. Haley, John W., *An Examination of the Alleged Discrepancies of the Bible*. Nashville: B. C. Goodpasture, 1953.

2. Packer, J. I., *Evangelism & The Sovereignty of God*. Downers Grove, Illinois: Inter Varsity Press, 1961.

3. Packer, J. I., *Knowing God*. Downers Grove, Illinois: Inter Varsity Press, 1973.

4. Boa, Kenneth, *God I Don't Understand*. Wheaton, Illinois: Victor Books, 1975.

# Republic of Texas Press

**Tragedy at Taos: The Revolt of 1847**
by James A. Crutchfield

**A Trail Rider's Guide to Texas**
by Mary Elizabeth Sue Goldman

**Unsolved Texas Mysteries**
by Wallace O. Chariton

**Western Horse Tales**
Edited by Don Worcester

**Wild Camp Tales**
by Mike Blakely

## Seaside Press

**The Bible for Busy People
Book 1: The Old Testament**
by Mark Berrier Sr.

**Critter Chronicles**
by Jim Dunlap

**Dallas Uncovered**
by Larenda Lyles Roberts

**Dirty Dining: A Cookbook, and More, for Lovers**
by Ginnie Siena Bivona

**Exotic Pets: A Veterinary Guide for Owners**
by Shawn Messonnier, D.V.M.

**I Never Wanted to Set the World on Fire, but Now That I'm 50, Maybe Its a Good Idea**
by Bob Basso, Ph.D.

**Just Passing Through**
by Beth Beggs

**Kingmakers**
by John R. Knaggs

**Lives and Works of the Apostles**
by Russell A. Stultz

**Los Angeles Uncovered**
by Frank Thompson

**Only: The Last Dinosaur**
by Jim Dunlap

**Seattle Uncovered**
by JoAnn Roe

**San Antonio Uncovered**
by Mark Louis Rybczyk

**A Sure Reward**
by B.J. Smagula

**Survival Kit for Today's Family**
by Bill R. Swetmon

**They Don't Have to Die**
by Jim Dunlap

**Twin Cities Uncovered**
by The Arthurs

**Your Puppy's First Year**
by Shawn Messonnier, D.V.M.

Call Wordware Publishing, Inc. for names of the bookstores in your area
(214) 423-0090